MW00809671

Love & Blessings,

Barbara Goodman Suigel

Praise for *Finding Your Self in the Mirror*

"With her excellent book, Finding Your Self in The Mirror, Barbara Goodman Siegel combines affirmations with the Workbook lessons of A Course in Miracles in such a way that will empower the reader to really get the meaning and experience the truth on an even deeper level than they would have. Whether you're a beginner student or an advanced one, internalizing these lessons will accelerate your spiritual journey. I highly recommend this important and timely book."

-Gary R. Renard
author of *The Disappearance of the Universe* trilogy

"Barbara Goodman Siegel has done a beautiful and inspired job of writing affirmations to help us work with our minds about our self-judgments and false perceptions. So helpful! When you actually take the time to work with these affirmations you will experience true and lasting transformation! Go for it!"

-Jennifer Helen Hadley
host of *A Course in Miracles* Radio Show at Unity FM
founder of *Living A Course in Miracles*

"Barbara Goodman Siegel provides a meaningful contribution to the efforts of Course students in deepening our experience with Spirit. The mirror affirmations help to personalize each lesson and encourage us to connect to our Divine Consciousness."

-Rev. Larry Glenz
author of *Forgiving Kevin: A Son's Addiction becomes a Father's Greatest Teacher*

"Taking these affirmations based on A Course in Miracles to the mirror on a daily basis, lifts my spirit and is helping me discover and embrace my true Self. I am using them to sign the lessons, and I can also use them for EFT! I am thankful to be blessed with this tool!"

-Rebecca Ebat
ministerial student, Pathways of Light

"This is a practice that brings the A Course in Miracles lessons literally face to face and front and center; stimulating and encouraging personal and practical application."

-John Hutkin
principal of Hutkin Development Co.

"Barbara's reflection exercises for the ACIM Workbook lessons is a truly helpful tool for students of ACIM, regardless of how long a person has been studying the Course. She has done an exceptional job of creating, with guidance, practical statements for each lesson to be stated in a mirroring exercise and then the perfect quotes from the ACIM Text to "affirm" the Truth. Anything that can help an ACIM student get from their head and into their heart has my support. I am so grateful for this new resource to actualize the message of the Course in one's daily life."

-Corinne Esneault
ACIM Study Group Leader
Attitudinal Healing St. Louis Facilitator

"In the mirror affirmations, Barbara brings the ACIM workbook lessons straight into the mind's eye, challenging us to engage with the illusion maker one on one, in the mirror, with eyes open. This book is an essential companion to A Course in Miracles".

-Amanda R. NcMichael
student of A Course in Miracles

"Barbara Goodman Siegel is among my favorite teachers of the Course. Her gift at healing perception is surpassed only by her kindness – and it comes through on every page."

-Emily Bennington
author of Miracles at Work: Turning Inner Guidance into Outer Influence

Finding Your *Self* in the Mirror

Awakening Through Mirror Affirmations
for the 365 Lessons of *A Course in Miracles*

Barbara Goodman Siegel

Copyright © 2017 by Barbara Goodman Siegel

Print ISBN: 978-1-54391-268-5
eBook ISBN: 978-1-54391-269-2

All rights reserved. No part of this book may be reproduced, scanned
or distributed in any printed or electronic form without permission.

Permission may be granted through the author, Barbara Goodman
Siegel, by e-mailing her at Barbara@BarbaraGoodmanSiegel.com

All quotes from **A Course in Miracles** are from the 2nd
Edition, ©Foundation for Inner Peace, PO Box 598, Mill Valley,
CA 949420598, www.acim.org and info@acim.org.

Introduction

Dearest fellow *A Course in Miracle* student,

The idea of this mirror work is to give us a tool to connect physically, psychologically, emotionally, and spiritually with our true Self as we do the workbook lessons.

I was guided to write this book for *Course* students of all levels; those who are doing the lessons for the first time, and those of us who have done the lessons several times over the years. One thing that the beginning student and the more "advanced" student may have in common is that the lessons can become an abstract, intellectual activity that we just keep in our head and never embody. We understand the lessons, we feel their beauty and power, but, for whatever reason, the lessons don't go deeper than the intellect.

Many of us stand outside the teachings of the lessons thinking we don't have what it takes to bring it into our hearts or that our challenges are too difficult to overcome. We tell ourselves that maybe someday when we have studied more, when our difficult challenges are resolved, etc., then we will be able to embody the lessons like *Course* teachers we admire.

I asked myself how this mistaken belief that only a chosen few could really "get it" could be changed. How could I change it for myself and other students? The answer came to me literally in the form of a series of daily mirror affirmations offered by Louise Hay and Hay House. The series had a different list of affirmations every day that you were to say out loud to yourself in-front of a mirror.

The Hay House Mirror Affirmation series I signed up for started Jan. 1, 2015, the same day I started the *Course* lessons again for the umpteenth time. After a week of doing the Hay House affirmations, it struck me (a real "ah ha" moment) that this practice of saying affirmations out loud in-front of the mirror would be a great practice for the *Course* lessons, and so I began to write the affirmations that you will see on the following pages. My practice was to get out of bed, get a cup of coffee and sit on the couch with my ACIM book, a legal pad and a pen. I read the daily lesson several times and just let myself "hear" what the affirmations should be for that lesson. It took the entire year of 2015 to complete the affirmations, basically doing one lesson a day as the *Course* instructs. When I began to type up the affirmations, I felt guided to include an appropriate quote from the text that would tie the text and the lesson together. I would read the lesson and ask Spirit to guide me to a quote. I almost always got to within a page or two of a perfect quote. When I felt I was struggling to find a good quote, I knew it was time to put the work down because I had moved from guidance to intellect.

The beginning lessons may be the most difficult, especially for the new student. I think of it as assembling the ingredients for a wonderful recipe knowing that each ingredient on its own does not make the dish. It is only as the ingredients are blended with each other does the recipe come together as a magnificent whole. So I ask you, dear reader, to have patience with the first lessons and know you are assembling the ingredients and the result will be beautiful beyond your wildest dreams.

If the affirmations I have received for a lesson don't feel right to you, then write your own. As we have been told in the *Course*, this course is personal, so let your higher Self be your guide in all you do.

I want to be very clear that this book was not written to replace reading the lessons in *A Course in Miracles*, but as a companion to the lessons. Nothing can replace the beauty, wisdom and guidance of the lessons as they are written and anyone who tries to find a shortcut around spending the time to read them will only be cheating themselves.

It is my deepest desire that you find the work I have done helpful to you as you do the lessons and that these lesson affirmations will be the bridge between your mind and your heart.

Love and Blessings,
Barbara

Instructions for Using the Mirror Affirmations with the Workbook Lessons of
A Course in Miracles

In getting the book ready to be published, I realized that the introduction may not give enough direction as to how to use the affirmations. Therefore, I have included some brief instructions below.

Before I proceed with the instructions, I want to say a few general things. First of all, if you just acquired this book, but you have already been doing the lessons in the *Course*, you do not have to start all over again. Just start the affirmations with the lesson number you are on. If you stay on a lesson for a few days, continue with the affirmations for that lesson. As with the *Course*, use this book in a way that makes it your own. Having a journal available for any affirmations you want to add or any insights you have would be very valuable.

Many beginners wonder if they did a few lessons and then put the book down for a few weeks or so, should they start all over. In general, I would say to pick-up where you left off. It may feel too discouraging if you think you have to keep going back to square one. That being said, always ask your Inner Guide what is right for you. If you feel at peace, then that is the right answer.

As for the rest:

1. Read the daily lesson that you are on in *A Course in Miracles*. Doing this in the morning before getting ready for the day would be the best time.

2. While you are getting dressed for the day, have the affirmations for that day's lesson in front of you. While you are looking in the mirror (drying your hair, shaving, putting on make-up, etc.) repeat the affirmations for the day's lesson.

3. I urge you to say the affirmations out-loud whenever possible to achieve the maximum effect.

4. During the day, when you are in-front of a mirror (washing your hands, combing your hair, etc.,) repeat the affirmations. Obviously, this will need to be done silently if you are in a public place.

5. At bedtime (while you are washing up, brushing your teeth, etc.), repeat the affirmations out-loud if possible.

6. Smile at yourself as you do this activity. Not only will this bring more joy to the activity, but it will also help you in acknowledging your true Self.

7. Never force something. I have used the words and masculine tense to stay consistent with the *Course.* If a word doesn't resonate with you, change it to what you are comfortable with.

8. If you feel uncomfortable about saying an affirmation, be aware of what voice (i.e., Inner Guide or ego) you are listening to. For example, the ego is not going to want you to look in the mirror, smile at yourself, and say: "I am holy" or "I am the innocent Son of God." This may feel uncomfortable at first, but keep going! Remember, the ego didn't have a problem looking in the mirror and saying the exact opposite and this is the voice you have listened to your whole live and it is not going to give up its dominance in your head easily!

9. If you feel stuck or in need of support, find out if there is a local *Course in Miracles* group in your area. Pathways of Light has several free conference call support groups. You can find more information on their website, www.pathwaysoflight.org.

10. I am here to support you however I can. I am happy to answer your questions by e-mail, or, if you would like to go deeper, support you with spiritual, one-on-one phone counseling. I am available to do one-on-one phone counseling anywhere within the United States.

Please feel free to e-mail me at Barbara@BarbaraGoodmanSiegel.com

Lesson 1

Nothing I see in this room (in this mirror) means anything.

1. Nothing I see in this mirror means anything

2. These eyes do not mean anything

3. This mouth does not mean anything

4. This body does not mean anything

5. I am happy to take this first step

6. In gratitude, I smile at myself for this beginning

"The ego's picture of you is deprived, unloving and vulnerable. You cannot love this. Yet you can very easily escape from this image by leaving it behind."
T-7.VII.3: 2-4

Lesson 2

I have given everything I see in this room (in this mirror) all the meaning it has for me.

1. I have given my eyes all the meaning they have for me
2. I have given this mouth all the meaning it has for me
3. I have given this body (arms, wrinkles, fat, breast, stomach, etc.) all the meaning it has for me
4. I am happy to realize this
5. In gratitude I smile at myself for taking this beginning

"Every response you make to everything you perceive is up to you, because your mind determines your perception of it."
T-10.In.2:7

Lesson 3

I do not understand anything I see in this room (mirror)

1. I do not understand these eyes

2. I do not understand this mouth

3. I do not understand this body

4. As I do not understand what I see in the world, I do not understand what I see in the mirror

5. I smile at myself in gratitude as I continue to move forward

---

"Grace is not given to a body, but to a mind. And the mind that receives it looks instantly beyond the body and sees the holy place where it was healed."
T-19.V1.13:1-2

Lesson 4

These thoughts do not mean anything. They are like the things I see in this room (mirror)

(Note: As you look in the mirror, become aware of thoughts such as: "I am really having a bad hair day; Wow! Look at those wrinkles around my eyes; I look fat; Why hasn't _____ called; What should I do about _____" etc.)

1. I smile at myself as I become aware of my thoughts
2. I smile and say: " this thought does not mean anything"
3. I am willing to release this thought
4. I release this thought as if it were a balloon and I let it float away
5. I am happy seeing my thoughts as nothing but balloons that I can release at will

---

"The ego's voice is an hallucination."
T-8.VI. 2:2

Lesson 5

I am never upset for the reason I think

1. I am not angry at _____ for the reason I think

2. I am not anxious about _____ for the reason I think

3. I am not feeling depressed about _____ for the reason I think

4. I am not jealous of _____ for the reason I think

5. All these forms of upset are like different colored balloons and they all make me feel separate and alone

6. I am willing to release them in-order to have peace of mind

7. I smile and thank myself for doing this work

"Let not the form of his mistakes keep you from him whose holiness is yours. Let not the vision of his holiness, the sight of which would show you your forgiveness, be kept from you by what the body's eyes can see. Let your awareness of your brother not be blocked by your perception of his sins and of his body." T-22.III.8:1-3

Lesson 6

I am upset because I see something that isn't there

("It is necessary to name both the form of upset and the perceived source very specifically for any application of the idea")

1. I am angry at _____ because I see something that isn't there

2. I am anxious about _____ because I see something that isn't there

3. I am depressed about _____ because I see something that isn't there

4. I am worried about _____ because I see something that isn't there

5. The only purpose of these forms of upset is to make me feel separate and alone

6. I am willing to release these feelings like colored balloons filled only with air

7. I smile as I watch them float away

"Do not allow yourself to suffer from imagined results of what is not true. Free your mind from the belief that this is possible."
T-8.VII.16:1-2

Lesson 7

I see only the past

1. I see only the past in these eyes

2. I see only the past in this body

3. I see only the past in these hands

4. I see only the past in everything reflected in this mirror

5. I am willing to release these past judgments of what I see in-order to have peace of mind

6. I am willing to release these past judgments in-order to find my true Self

7. In gratitude I smile at myself for this beginning

"It is as needful that you recognize you made the world you see, as that you recognize that you did not create yourself. *They are the same mistake.*"
T-21.II.1-2

Lesson 8

My mind is preoccupied with past thoughts

Looking in the mirror, I seem to be thinking about (name of person, object and/or emotion), but my mind is preoccupied with past thoughts

1. I smile as I recognize this truth
2. I release the thought and see it float away
3. I am having fun learning this
4. I smile at myself in joy and appreciation

"In the holy instant it is understood that the past is gone, and with its passing the drive for vengeance has been uprooted and has disappeared. The stillness and the peace of now enfold you in perfect gentleness. Everything is gone except the truth."
T-16.VII.6:4-6

Lesson 9

I see nothing as it is now

1. I do not see this face as it is now

2. I do not see these eyes as they are now

3. I do not see this mouth as it is now

4. I do not recognize my beauty as it is now

5. I smile in honor of the image I see now

6. I am grateful for my willingness to practice

"The ego uses the body for attack, for pleasure and for pride. The insanity of this perception makes it a fearful one indeed. The Holy Spirit sees the body only as a means of communication, and because communicating is sharing it becomes communion."
T-6:V.A.5:3-5

Lesson 10

My thoughts do not mean anything

1. (Looking in the mirror) I realize that my thought about my body does not mean anything

2. My thought about my face does not mean anything

3. My thought about my hair does not mean anything

4. I remember that "This idea will help release me from all I now believe."

5. I am willing to be released from these meaningless thoughts

6. I smile at myself as I let them go

7. I know I am preparing for true vision

8. I am grateful for my continued willingness to practice

"Give up gladly everything that would stand in the way of your remembering, for God is in your memory. "
T-10.II.2:4

Lesson 11

My meaningless thoughts are showing me a meaningless world

1. Looking at yourself in the mirror, slowly repeat several times: My meaningless thoughts about what I see are showing me a meaningless self.

2. I am glad to know this

3. I remember that I have given everything I see all the meaning it has for me

4. I am happy to release these meaningless thoughts

5. I know that all these thoughts about myself, my body, my worth, and my judgment thoughts about the thoughts I have are meaningless

6. I honor myself and God by doing this work

"Every miracle is but the end of an illusion. Such was the journey; such its ending. And in the goal of truth which you accepted must all illusions end."
T-19.IV. A.6:8-10

Lesson 12

I am upset because I see a meaningless world

1. I am fearful (depressed, angry, anxious)
   because I fear that I am meaningless
2. I am fearful because I believe the world
   I see is dangerous and hostile
3. I am willing to let these beliefs go like balloons
   that have been untethered from their anchor
4. I recognize that I created meaningless illusion
   about myself and the world around me
5. I am willing to accept the truth

"The whole purpose of this course is to teach you that the ego is unbelievable and will forever be unbelievable. "
T-7.VIII.7:1

Lesson 13

A meaningless world engenders fear

1. I have created my ego self out of fear
2. I am willing to release it to find the true Self created by God
3. I do not need to live with fear and anxiety
4. God does not want this for me
5. I give Him all my meaningless thoughts about myself and the world
6. I want the peace of God more than my illusions

"Nothing real can be threatened. Nothing unreal exists. Herein lies the peace of God."
Preface: p. 10

Lesson 14

God did not create a meaningless world

1. God did not create me to be meaningless

2. I made this meaningless self

3. I created fear and anxiety with illusions
   of what could happen to me

4. None of this was created by God

5. I am willing to allow the truth of God to be revealed to me

6. I love and honor myself for continuing to practice these ideas

---

"Fear and love are the only emotions of which you are capable."
T-12.I.9-5

Lesson 15

My thoughts are images I have made

1. I have used these eyes to form images based on the illusions of my thoughts

2. This face is an illusion I have made

3. This body is an illusion I have made

4. I want to see beyond my illusions

5. I want to see truth

6. I am starting to see with my spiritual eye rather then my bodies eye

7. I am grateful to know the difference

"Spiritual vision looks within and recognizes immediately that the altar has been defiled and needs to be repaired and protected." T-2.III.4:3

Lesson 16

I have no neutral thoughts

1. This thought about my face is not a neutral thought
2. This thought about my hair is not a neutral thought
3. This thought about my body is not a neutral thought
4. There is nothing I see in this mirror that I have not given meaning to
5. I am willing to set aside all my judgments and opinions for peace
6. I am willing to love myself

"It is still up to you to choose to join with truth or with illusion. But remember that to choose one is to let the other go. Which one you choose you will endow with beauty and reality, because the choice depends on which you value more."
T-17.III.9:1-3

Lesson 17

I see no neutral things

1. "I see no neutral things because I have no neutral thoughts"

2. I do not see a neutral face (nose, eyes, etc.) because my thoughts about my face are not neutral

3. I do not see a neutral body (arms, breasts, stomach, etc.) because my thoughts about my body are not neutral

4. I am starting to see how all my thoughts have separated me from the truth of who I am

5. I honor myself for continuing to do these lessons

"No one can escape from illusions unless he looks at them, for not looking is the way they are protected."
T–11.V.1:1

Lesson 18

I am not alone in experiencing the effects of my seeing

1. I am not alone in experiencing the effects of how I see this face (eyes, mouth, breast, etc.)
2. I am not alone in how I see myself or my thoughts
3. I am not alone in experiencing the effects of my perceptions
4. What I see I project into the world
5. I want to see God's peace and beauty

"You see what you expect, and you expect what you invite. Your perception is the result of your invitation, coming to you as you sent for it. Whose manifestations would you see?"
T-12.VII.5:1-3

Lesson 19

I am not alone in experiencing the effects of my thoughts

1. I am not alone in experiencing the effects of my thoughts about myself

2. My mind is joined with my brothers

3. I have no private thoughts

4. If I see myself as (ugly, unworthy, guilty, etc.), I cannot help but project this energy out

5. I am willing to release these thoughts

6. I am open to learning God's truth in place of mine

"All your difficulties stem from the fact you do not recognize yourself, your brother or God."
T-3.III.2:1

Lesson 20

I am determined to see

1. I am determined to see differently
2. I want salvation
3. I want to be happy
4. I want peace
5. I am willing to discipline my mind
6. I am determined to see as God would want me to see

"Atonement becomes real and visible to those who use it. On earth this is your only function and you must learn that it is all you want to learn."
T-14.IV.3:6-7

Lesson 21

I am determined to see things differently

1. I am determined to see this body differently

2. I am determined to see myself differently

3. I am determined to see (name of person) differently

4. I am determined to see (situation) differently

5. I am determined to release my attack thoughts about myself and others

6. I am worthy

7. I am grateful for these lessons

"What you have made is so unworthy of you that you could hardly want it, if you were willing to see it as it is."
T-10.IV.5:7

Lesson 22

What I see is a form of vengeance

1. My attack thoughts about myself and others represent all my stored anger

2. My thoughts of vengeance represent my fear of vengeance coming back on me

3. I have created this vicious cycle out of my illusions

4. I am willing to release it

5. My awareness is the first step

6. I am willing and grateful to have this awareness

"You are the dreamer of the world of dreams. No other cause it has, nor ever will. Nothing more fearful than an idle dream has terrified God's Son, and made him think that he has lost his innocence, denied his Father, and made war upon himself."
T–27.VII.13:1-3

Lesson 23

I can escape from the world I see by giving up attack thoughts

1. I can escape from the world I see by giving up attack thoughts about myself (my looks, worthiness, intelligence, etc.)

2. I can escape from the world I see by giving up attack thoughts about (name)

3. I can escape from the world I see by giving up thoughts that (name) is attacking me (because of my looks, worthiness, intelligence, etc.)

4. I take a deep breath and release the thought

5. In my mind I see the black balloon of attack floating away and I smile

6. I am peaceful

7. I am loving

"The ego always attacks on behalf of separation."
T–11.V.7:1

Lesson 24

I do not perceive in my own best interest

1. I think I know what will make me happy

2. I am willing to admit I do not know what will make me happy

3. I thought I would be happy when (situation) happened but that happiness quickly faded

4. I think I will be happy when (situation) happens, but it will be like the past

5. I do not perceive in my own best interest

6. I am opening my mind to a different way of perceiving

7. I am open to the happiness God wants for me

"Yet I do want to share my mind with you because we are of one Mind, and that Mind is ours. See only this Mind everywhere because only this is everywhere and in everything. It is everything because it encompasses all things within itself. Blessed are you who perceive only this, because you perceive only what is true."
T-7.V.10:9-12

Lesson 25

I do not know what anything is for

1. I do not know what anything I see in this mirror is for

2. My ego has given everything I see in this mirror its meaning

3. My true Self is not my ego

4. I am willing to give up the goals I have established for everything

5. These goals are not good or bad but meaningless

6. I am determined to see Truth

"Reality cannot breakthrough the obstructions you interpose, but it will envelop you completely when you let them go."
T-10.IV.5:10

Lesson 26

My attack thoughts are attacking my invulnerability

1. I project attack thoughts
2. I feel my attack thoughts are justified
3. I fear that what I attacked will attack me
4. I am making myself feel fearful, guilty, depressed and vulnerable
5. I am willing to give up my attack thoughts
6. I am stronger and safer without these attack thoughts
7. I am purifying my mind

"The mind that accepts attack cannot love. That is because it believes it can destroy love, and therefore does not understand what love is."
T-7.VI.2:1-2

Lesson 27

Above all else I want to see

1. I would not have come this far if this were not true

2. Above all else I want to see

3. This desire is deep within me

4. I honor it

5. It can only bless

6. Above all else I want to see

"And you will see me as you look within, and we will look upon the real world together."
T–12.VII.11:6

Lesson 28

Above all else I want to see things differently

1. I want to see what is now

2. I want to see without the past

3. I want to see this face differently

4. I want to see this body (etc.) differently

5. I want to see with love

"Perception is a choice of what you want yourself to be: the world you want to live in, and the state in which you think your mind will be content and satisfied."
T–28.I.3:1

Lesson 29

God is in everything I see

1. God is in this face
2. God is in this hand
3. God is in this body
4. God is in this sink
5. God is in everything I see
6. I smile at myself knowing God is within me

"Never forget the Love of God, Who has remembered you. For it is quite impossible that He could ever let His Son drop from the loving Mind wherein he was created and where his abode was fixed in perfect peace forever."
T-14.III.15:7-8

Lesson 30

God is in everything I see because God is in my mind

1. God is in my mind

2. Love is in my mind because God is in my mind

3. Peace is in my mind because God is in my mind

4. Holiness is in my mind because God is in my mind

5. Healing is in my mind because God is in my mind

6. All this is what I want to see

"You are a mirror of truth, in which God Himself shines in perfect light."
T–4.IV.9:1

Lesson 31

I am not the victim of the world I see

1. I am not the victim of the world I see

2. I am not the victim of the world I see

3. I am not the victim of the world I see

4. I am not the victim of the thoughts in my mind

5. This is my declaration of independence

6. This is my declaration of freedom

7. I am not the victim of the world I see

"Therefore, seek not to change the world, but choose to change your mind about the world. Perception is a result and not a cause. And that is why order of difficulty in miracles is meaningless. Everything looked upon with vision is healed and holy."
T–21.In.1:7-10

Lesson 32

I have invented the world I see

1. I have invented each thing I see in this mirror
2. I have invented a label for each thing
   (Good, bad, pretty, ugly, etc.)
3. I have invented each thought that goes through my mind
4. I have invented a label for each thought
   (Good, bad, loving, fearful, etc.)
5. I have invented every situation as I see it and I have made myself either the victim or the hero
6. I am willing to release everything I have invented to my higher Self to be purified from my illusions
7. Thank you dear God for your support in all I do

"The necessary condition for the holy instant does not require that you have no thoughts that are not pure. But it does require that you have none that you would keep."
T–15.IV.9:1-2

Lesson 33

There is another way of looking at the world

1. I am aware that everything I see is
   filtered through my judgments

2. I am aware that everything I think is
   filtered through my judgments

3. I am willing to release my judgments to my higher Self

4. There is another way of looking at the world

5. Above all else, I want to see Truth

"You perceive from your mind and project your perceptions outward. Although perception of any kind is unreal, you made it and the Holy Spirit can therefore use it well. He can inspire perception and lead it toward God."
T-6.II.9:5-7

Lesson 34

I could see peace instead of this

1. I let go of my attack thoughts

2. My peace is in my mind

3. I want a peaceful mind

4. My peaceful mind will make a peaceful world

5. In all things today I remind myself: "I could see peace instead of this"

6. With deep breath of gratitude, I give thanks for this knowing

---

"When your peace is threatened or disturbed in any way, say to yourself:

I do not know what anything, including this means. And so I do not know how to respond to it. And I will not use my own past learning as the light to guide me now."
T–14.XI.6:6-9

Lesson 35

My mind is part of God's. I am very holy

1. God is my Source

2. Through the Love of God I am created

3. In each moment I am held by His Love

4. My mind is part of God's

5. I am very holy

6. In this moment I release my illusions and accept the truth of who I am

7. I am God's holy child held eternally in His Love

"*You* are the means for God; not separate, nor with a life apart from His. His life is manifest in you who are His Son."
T–25.I.4: 1-2

Lesson 36

My holiness envelops everything I see

1. I am holy

2. I am the innocent child of God

3. He has given me all that He is

4. I see with His holiness and His holiness is in everything I see

5. Nothing is separate from Him

6. All is one

"In you is all of Heaven. Every leaf that falls is given life in you. Each bird that ever sang will sing again in you. And every flower that ever bloomed has saved its perfume and its loveliness for you."
T–25.IV.5:1-4

Lesson 37

My holiness blesses the world

1. My purpose is to see the world through my own holiness

2. My purpose is to bless all my brothers equally

3. My holiness is the salvation of the world

4. I am blessed as I bless

5. All is one

6. In love and gratitude I willingly accept my purpose

"In the holy instant the Sonship gains as one, and united in your blessing it becomes one to you."
T15.V.10:2

Lesson 38

There is nothing my holiness cannot do

1. I was created by God

2. I am holy

3. Through my holiness the power of God is made manifest

4. Through my holiness the power of God is made available

5. I am willing to bring holiness to all I see

6. I am humbled to know the power of God works through me

"To accept yourself as God created you cannot be arrogance, because it is the denial of arrogance. To accept your littleness is arrogant, because it means that you believe your evaluation of yourself is truer than God's."
T-9.VIII.10:8-9

Lesson 39

My holiness is my salvation

1. I was created by God
2. I am holy
3. I created my guilt, not God
4. What is not of God is not real
5. Guilt is not real
6. I am willing to let my unloving thoughts go
7. I am the holy, innocent Self, the Son of God

"Little child, innocent of sin, follow in gladness the way
to certainty."
T-21.IV.8:3

Lesson 40

I am blessed as a Son of God

1. I am happy as a Son of God

2. I am calm as a Son of God

3. I am abundant as a Son of God

4. I am peaceful as a Son of God

5. I am confident as a Son of God

6. I am blessed as a Son of God

7. I am grateful as a Son of God

"He to Whom time is given offers thanks for every quiet instant given Him. For in that instant is God's memory allowed to offer all its treasures to the Son of God, for whom they have been kept." T-28.I.12:1-2

Lesson 41

God goes with me wherever I go

1. I am not alone

2. I am not separate

3. I am all that God would have me be

4. I am the perfect Son of God

5. I am holy

6. I am at peace

7. I am loved

"I am teaching you to associate misery with the ego and joy with the spirit."
T-4.VI.5:6

Lesson 42

God is my strength. Vision is His gift.

1. I will see because it is the Will of God
2. God's strength gives me power
3. God's gift of vision allows me to see
4. I will not question God's will for me
5. I accept His gift with gratitude
6. Thank you God for Your strength and for Your vision

"*You* are the means for God; not separate, nor with a life apart from His. His life is manifest in you who are His Son."
T–25.I.4:1-2

Lesson 43

God is my Source. I cannot see apart from Him

1. God is my Source

2. I cannot leave my Source

3. I am eternally connected to God through my higher Self

4. Through my higher Self, I see the world Forgiven

5. Through my higher Self, I see the world blessed

6. With my higher Self, I cannot see apart from God

7. With my higher Self, I cannot see my brother apart from God

8. We are one

"I thank You, Father, for Your perfect Son, and in his glory will I see my own."
T–30.VI.9:4

Lesson 44

God is the light in which I see

1. I see myself as holy
2. I see myself as blessed
3. I see the world blessed
4. I see the world forgiven
5. I see through my spiritual eye
6. I see with the holy light of God

"Joy cannot be perceived except through constant vision. And constant vision can be given only those who wish for constancy."
T-21.VII.13:3-4

Lesson 45

God is the Mind with which I think

1. I am one with God, my Source

2. I cannot think apart from Him

3. I am holy

4. My mind is holy

5. Only the thoughts I think with my higher Self are real

6. I accept my holiness with deep humility and gratitude

"And not one Thought that God has ever had but waited for your blessing to be born."
T–30.II.1:10

Lesson 46

God is the Love in which I forgive

1. I am willing to release my illusions of guilt and blame

2. I am willing to see things differently

3. I see with the light of God

4. With the Love of God, I forgive my brother

5. With the Love of God, I forgive myself

6. With the Love of God, I love myself

7. God is the Love in which I am blessed

"Perhaps you do not see the need for you to give this little offering. Look closer, then, at what it is. And, very simply, see in it the whole exchange of separation for salvation."
T–21.II.6:1-3

Lesson 47

God is the strength in which I trust

1. Of myself I can do nothing

2. With the strength of God I can do anything

3. God is my safety in all circumstances

4. God's Voice will direct me as to what to do, what to say and to whom

5. I am never apart from God's strength

6. I am at peace

7. Thank you, dear God, for your strength, your love and your light

---

"In His link with you lie both His inability to forget and your ability to remember. In Him are joined your willingness to love and all the Love of God, Who forgot you not."
T–16.IV.II:13-14

Lesson 48

There is nothing to fear

1. I willingly give up my illusions

2. There is nothing to fear

3. Only the thoughts I think with God are real

4. There is nothing to fear

5. God is the strength in which I trust

6. There is nothing to fear

"Every illusion is one of fear, whatever form it takes."
T–16.IV.6:3

Lesson 49

God's Voice speaks to me all through the day

1. Part of my mind is in constant communication with God
2. I listen to Him with my spiritual ear
3. I quiet my worldly ear
4. I am training my undisciplined mind
5. I lovingly keep turning my mind back to God
6. Here is my peace
7. Here is my true home

"Both Heaven and earth are in you, because the call of both is in your mind. The Voice for God comes from your own altars to Him."
T-5.II.8:5-6

Lesson 50

I am sustained by the Love of God

1. I am supported by the Love of God

2. I am protected by the Love of God

3. I am created by the Love of God

4. I am comforted by the Love of God

5. I am led by the Love of God

6. I am lifted by the Love of God

7. I am the Love of God

"That is how God Himself created you; in understanding, in appreciation and in love."
T–7.V.9:5

Review I

Dear one:

We now begin the review of the first 50 lessons. As stated in the introduction to the review: "We are now emphasizing the relationships among the first fifty of the ideas we have covered, and the cohesiveness of the thought system to which they are leading you." Again, I want to emphasize that these mirror exercises are not to replace reading through the lessons as they are written in the workbook, the introduction to the reviews, and the reviews themselves. You will find that the short explanation for each lesson in the review is different than the original explanation given when the lesson was first introduced. Carefully reading the review's explanation will go far in helping you to weave this new thought system together.

I have repeated my favorite sentence from each review lesson as the affirmation for the lesson. Your favorite sentence may be different than mine and I invite you to find the sentence that speaks to you to repeat for your affirmation. You may also want to write them in your journal.

Lesson 51

1. (1) **Nothing I see means anything**: What I think I see now takes the place of vision.

2. (2) **I have given what I see all the meaning it has for me:** I have judged everything I look upon.

3. (3) **I do not understand anything I see**: What I see is the projection of my own errors of thought.

4. (4) **These thoughts do not mean anything**: My real thoughts are the thoughts I think with God

5. (5) **I am never upset for the reason I think**: I make all things my enemies, so that my anger is justified and my attacks are warranted. I have done this to defend a thought system that has hurt me and I no longer want. I am willing to let it go.

"This is a course in mind training. All learning involves attention and study at some level."
T–1:VII.4:1-2

My favorite sentences in these review lessons are:

Lesson 52

1. (6) **I am upset because I see what is not there**: Reality brings only perfect peace.

2. (7) **I see only the past**: Without the past, I look with love on all that I failed to see before.

3. (8) **My mind is preoccupied with past thoughts**: I am willing to give the past away, realizing that in so doing I am giving up nothing.

4. (9) **I see nothing as it is now**: Now I would choose again that I may see.

5. (10) **My thoughts do not mean anything**: My mind is part of creation and part of its Creator.

"Your divided mind is blocking the extension of the Kingdom and its extension is your joy."
T-7.VI.12:4

My favorite sentences in these review lessons are:

_____

_____

_____

Lesson 53

1. (11) **My meaningless thoughts are showing me a meaningless world**
   I have real thoughts as well as insane ones. I
   can therefore see a real world, if I look to my
   real thoughts as my guide for seeing.

2. (12) **I am upset because I see a meaningless world**:
   I do not choose to value what is totally
   insane and has no meaning.

3. (13) **A meaningless world engenders fear**:
   Now, I choose to withdraw my belief in this
   insane world, and place my trust in reality.

4. (14) **God did not create a meaningless world**:
   God is the Source of all meaning, and everything that
   is real is in His Mind. It (therefore) is in my mind, too.

5. (15) **My thoughts are images that I have made**:
   God's way is sure. My will is His, and I will
   place no other gods before Him.

"There is no barrier between God and His Son, nor can His Son
be separated from Himself except in illusions."
T–18.VI.9:3

My favorite sentences in these review lessons are:

_____

_____

_____

Lesson 54

1. (16) **I have no neutral thoughts:**
   As the world I see arises from my thinking errors, so will the real world rise before my eyes as I let my errors be corrected.

2. (17) **I see no neutral things:**
   I know that my state of mind can change. And so I know the world I see can change as well.

3. (18) **I am not alone in experiencing the effects of my seeing:**
   As my thoughts of separation call to the separation thoughts of others, so my real thoughts awaken the real thoughts in them.

4. (19) **I am not alone in experiencing the effects of my thoughts:**
   Everything I think or say or do teaches all the universe.

5. (20) **I am determined to see:**
   I would behold proof that what has been done through me has enabled love to replace fear, laughter to replace tears, and abundance to replace loss.

"You cannot enter God's Presence if you attack His Son."
T–11.IV.5:6

My favorite sentences in these review lessons are:

_____

_____

_____

Lesson 55

1. (21) **I am determined to see things differently:**
   I am determined to see the witnesses to the truth in me,
   rather than those which show me an illusion of myself

2. (22) **What I see is a form of vengeance:**
   My loving thoughts will save me from this perception of the
   world, and give me the peace God intended me to have.

3. (23) **I can escape from this world by giving up attach
   thoughts:**
   Herein lies my salvation and nowhere else.

4. (24) **I do not perceive my own best interest:**
   I am willing to follow the Guide God has given me
   to find out what my own best interests are.

5. (25) **I do not know what anything is for:**
   Let me open my mind to the world's real
   purpose by withdrawing the one I have given
   it, and learning the truth about it.

"Faith and belief and vision are the means by which the goal of
holiness is reached."

T–21.III.4:1

My favorite sentences in these review lessons are:

_____

_____

_____

Lesson 56

1. (26) **My attack thoughts are attacking my invulnerability**:
    Perfect security and complete fulfilment are my inheritance.

2. (27) **Above all else I want to see**:
    If I would remember who I am, it is essential
    that I let this image of myself go.

3. (28) **Above all else I want to see differently**:
    I would let the door behind this world be opened for me, that
    I may look past it to the world that reflects the Love of God.

4. (29) **God is in everything I see**:
    And we who are part of Him will yet look past all
    appearances, and recognize the truth beyond them all.

5. (30) **God is in everything I see because God is in my mind**:
    In my own mind, behind all my insane thoughts of separation
    and attack, is the knowledge that all is one forever.

"The whole value of right perception lies in the inevitable
realization that all perception is unnecessary."
T–4.II.11:3

My favorite sentences in these review lessons are:

_____

_____

_____

Lesson 57

1. (31) **I am not the victim of the world I see**
    My chains are loosened. I give up my insane
    wishes and walk into the sunlight at last.

2. (32) **I have invented the world I see**:
    I made up the prison in which I see myself.
    I recognize this and I am free.

3. (33) **There is another way of looking at the world**:
    The world is a place where the Son of God finds his freedom.

4. (34) **I could see peace instead of this**:
    And I will perceive that peace also abides in the
    hearts of all who share this place with me.

5. (35) **My mind is part of God's. I am very holy:**
    I begin to understand the holiness of all living things,
    including myself, and their oneness with me.

"Look gently on your brother, and behold the world in which
perception of your hate has been transformed into a world
of love."
T–26.V.14:5

My favorite sentences in these review lessons are:

_____

_____

_____

Lesson 58

1. (36) **My holiness envelops everything I see**:
   I no longer see myself as guilty. I accept the
   innocence that is the truth about me.

2. (37) **My holiness blesses the world:**
   Everyone and everything I see in its light
   shares in the joy it brings to me.

3. (38) **There is nothing my holiness cannot do:**
   My holiness is unlimited in its power to heal,
   because it is unlimited in its power to save.

4. (39) **My holiness is my salvation:**
   Since my holiness saves me from all guilt, recognizing
   my holiness is recognizing my salvation.

5. (40) **I am blessed as a Son of God**:
   My Father supports me, protects me
   and directs me in all thing

"Healing, then, is a way of approaching knowledge by
thinking in accordance with the laws of God, and recognizing
their universality."
T–7.II.6:9

My favorite sentences in these review lessons are:

_____

_____

_____

Lesson 59

1. (41) **God goes with me wherever I go:**
   How can I be alone when God always goes with me?

2. (42) **God is my strength. Vision is His gift:**
   Let me be willing to exchange my pitiful illusion
   of seeing for the vision that is given by God.

3. (43) **God is my Source. I cannot see apart from Him:**
   I can see what God wants me to see

4. (44) **God is the light in which I see:**
   Let me welcome vision and the happy world it will show me

5. (45) **God is the Mind with which I think:**
   I have no thoughts I do not share with God

"The truth in you remains as radiant as a star, as pure as light,
as innocent as love itself. And you *are* worthy that your will
be done!"
T–31.VI.7:4-5

My favorite sentences in these review lessons are:

_____

_____

_____

Lesson 60

1. (46) **God is the Love in which I forgive**:
   Yet forgiveness is the means by which I
   will recognize my innocence.

2. (47) **God is the strength in which I trust**:
   I forgive all things because I feel the
   stirring of His strength in me.

3. (48) **There is nothing to fear**:
   What could there be to fear in a world that I
   have forgiven, and that has forgiven me?

4. (49) **God's Voice speaks to me all through the day**:
   There is not a moment in which His Voice fails to direct
   my thoughts, guide my actions, and lead my feet.

5. (50) **I am sustained by the Love of God**:
   As I open my eyes, His Love lights up the world for me to see.

"How beautiful it is to walk clean and redeemed and happy
through a world in bitter need of the redemption that your
innocence bestows upon it!"
T–23.Intro.6:5

My favorite sentences in these review lessons are:

_____

_____

_____

Lesson 61

I am the light of the world

1. I am God's Son
2. I am the light of the world
3. This is my only function
4. This is why I am here
5. I bless the world with my light
6. My light is very holy
7. God is my eternal Source of light

"In your relationship you have joined with me in bringing Heaven to the Son of God, who hid in darkness. You have been willing to bring the darkness to light, and this willingness has given strength to everyone who would remain in darkness."
T–18.III.6:1-2

Lesson 62

Forgiveness is my function as the light of the world

1. Forgiveness lets me recognize the light in which I see

2. As I forgive my Self returns to my memory

3. In my forgiveness lies my salvation

4. My forgiveness is a gift I give to myself

5. My beliefs in my fear and guilt and pain
   are released by my forgiveness

6. Forgiveness is my function as the light of the world

7. I would fulfill my function that I may be happy

"You must forgive God's Son entirely. Or you will keep an image of yourself that is not whole, and will remain afraid to look within and find escape from every idol there."
T–VI.7:5-6

Lesson 63

The light of the world brings peace to every mind through my forgiveness

1. I am holy

2. I am blessed

3. I have the power to bring peace to every mind

4. I am the light of the world

5. I accept salvation so that I may give it

6. My Self is God's Son

"No darkness abides anywhere in the Kingdom, but your part is only to allow no darkness to abide in your own mind. This alignment with light is unlimited, because it is in alignment with the light of the world. Each of us is the light of the world, and by joining our minds in this light we proclaim the Kingdom of God together and as one."
T–6.II.13:3-5

Lesson 64

Let me not forget my function

1. I am worthy of the function given me by God

2. I am the Son of God

3. My happiness lies only in fulfilling my function

4. Let me not forget my function

5. Let me not try to substitute mine for God's

6. Let me forgive and be happy

7. Thank you God for Your support and guidance in all I do

"Teach only love, for that is what you are."
T–6.I.13:2

Lesson 65

My only function is the one God gave me

1. I am committed to salvation

2. Salvation is my only function

3. Salvation is the function God gave me

4. By fulfilling my function I find peace of mind

5. By fulfilling my function I find happiness

6. My only function is the one God gave me. I want no other and I have no other.

7. I am worthy

"He would have you replace the ego's belief in littleness with His Own exalted Answer to what you are so that you can cease to question it and know it for what it is."
T–9.VIII.11:9

Lesson 66

My happiness and my function are one

1. God gives me only happiness
2. (Therefore) my function must be happiness
3. I am willing to release my fear
4. I allow the Love that I am to replace it
5. I choose to listen to truth
6. My happiness and my function are one

"God is with you, my brother. Let us join in Him in peace and gratitude, and accept His gift as our most holy and perfect reality, which we share in Him."
T–18.I.10: 8-9

Lesson 67

Love created me like itself

1. I am love

2. I am kindness

3. I am truth

4. I am light

5. I am that I am

6. I am the higher, holy Self that God created

7. I am whole

"When you perceive yourself without deceit, you will accept the real world in place of the false one you have made. And then your Father will lean down to you and take the last step for you, by raising you unto Himself."
T-11.VIII.15:4-5

Lesson 68

Love holds no grievances

1. I was created by Love

2. My true Self is held eternally in love

3. My grievances keep me separate from my Self

4. I am willing to release guilt and anger

5. Above all else I want peace

6. Above all else I want to know my Self

"When you want only love you will see nothing else. The contradictory nature of the witnesses you perceive is merely the reflection of your conflicting invitations."
T–12.VII.8:1-2

Lesson 69

My grievances hide the light of the world in me

1. My grievances weave a veil that conceal my light
2. I willingly lift the veil
3. I willingly stand in my light
4. I willingly see the light in all my brothers
5. Here is my salvation
6. Here is the salvation of the world
7. Here I am one with God

"Be humble before Him, and yet great *in* Him. And value no plan of the ego before the plan of God."
T–15.IV.3:1-2

Lesson 70

My salvation comes from me

1. My guilt is an invention of my mind
2. My salvation is in my mind
3. I am in charge of the universe
4. Every grievance is a cloud made of guilt
5. God wants my healing
6. I willingly move beyond the clouds into the light
7. In the light is my salvation

"You have no idea of the tremendous release and deep peace that comes from meeting yourself and your brothers totally without judgment."
T–3.VI.3:1

Lesson 71

Only God's plan for salvation will work

1. I want salvation

2. I want peace

3. I am willing to give up my grievances of blame and guilt

4. I accept God's plan for salvation

5. All things are possible to God

6. My salvation is God's Truth

7. I am willing to hear God's Voice instead of my own

"The whole purpose of this course is to teach you that the ego is unbelievable and will forever be unbelievable."
T–7.VIII.7:1

Lesson 72

Holding grievances is an attack on God's plan for salvation

1. I am not a body
2. My brother is not a body
3. God's truth is oneness
4. I am one with my brothers
5. We are one in the Mind of God
6. God's plan for salvation has already been accomplished in me
7. What is whole in God cannot hold grievances

"Love calls, but hate would have you stay. Hear not the call of hate and see no fantasies. For your completion lies in truth and nowhere else."
T–16.IV.11:3-5

Lesson 73

I will there be light

1. The will I share with God has all the power of creation in it
2. I willingly release judgments
3. I willingly release grievances
4. I will not block my true Self
5. I will succeed because I want salvation
6. It is my will to be happy
7. May God's will and my will be one

"Let us join in Him in peace and gratitude, and accept His gift as our most holy and perfect reality, which we share in Him."
T–18.I.10:9

Lesson 74

There is no will but God's

1. Only God's will is real

2. I cannot be in conflict

3. I share God's will

4. God's will is peace and so is mine

5. God's will is love and so is mine

6. We are one

"All real pleasure comes from doing God's Will. This is because *not* doing it is a denial of Self."
T–1.VII.1:4-5

Lesson 75

The light has come

1. I am healed
2. I can heal
3. I am saved
4. I can save
5. I bring peace with me wherever I go
6. I have forgiven the world
7. Thank you dear God for Your mercy and Your love

"What you forgot was simply that God cannot destroy Himself. The light is *in* you. Darkness can cover it, but cannot put it out." T- 18.III.1:6-8

Lesson 76

I am under no law but God's

1. There are no laws except the laws of God

2. I am free

3. I am the channel for God's creation

4. I am the channel for God's love

5. I am the channel for God's joy

6. I am the channel for God's light

7. I was created worthy of being God's messenger

"Complexity is not of God. How could it be, when all He knows is one? He knows of one creation, one reality, one truth and but one Son. Nothing conflicts with oneness."
T–26.III.1:1-4

Lesson 77

I am entitled to miracles

1. I am entitled to miracles because I am God's Son

2. I receive miracles because that is God's wish

3. I offer miracles because I am one with God

4. My worthiness of miracles was ensured in my creation

5. I am released from the world I made

6. Within me is the Kingdom of God

"Thank God that He is there and works through you. And all His works are yours. He offers you a miracle with every one you let Him do through you."
T–14.XI.10:7-10

Lesson 78

Let miracles replace all grievances

1. Every decision I make is between a grievance and a miracle

2. My grievance puts a dark shield of hate before my eyes

3. I am willing to lay down my shield

4. I am willing to free myself and my brother

5. Now can I see God's holy light

6. Now am I saved to save the world

"In this world you can become a spotless mirror, in which the Holiness of your Creator shines forth from you to all around you. You can reflect Heaven here."
T–14.IX.5:1-2

Lesson 79

Let me recognize the problem so it can be solved

1. My only problem is separation
2. My problem is solved
3. I am one with God
4. I am one with all God's Sons
5. I am free
6. I am at peace

"Healing is the way in which the separation is overcome.
Separation is overcome by union."
T–8.IV.5:3-4

Lesson 80

Let me recognize my problems have been solved

1. My only problem is solved

2. I am not separate from God

3. I am not separate from my higher Self

4. I am at peace

5. I am free

6. I am grateful

"Yet to the dedication to the truth as God established it no sacrifice is asked, no strain called forth, and all the power of Heaven and the might of truth itself is given to provide the means, and guarantee the goal's accomplishment."
T–24.VI.12:5

Review II

Dear one:

It is very important to carefully read the introduction to these next review lessons from your ACIM book. In paragraph 3 of the introduction, it says: "There is a message waiting for you. Be confident that you will receive it. Remember that it belongs to you, and that you want it." Therefore, after every review lesson, I have included a reminder for you to write your message in your journal. As you go through the day and do your affirmations, other messages may come. Be sure and write them down them as well. We often want to question if the message is from the Divine or our ego, particularly if the message is loving and beautiful. Be assured it is from the Divine! Do not judge the message, just write it down and trust that your higher Self is talking with you. It has wanted this opportunity for a very long time.

Lesson 81

Morning review

(61) I am the light of the world

1. I am holy
2. God's light shines through me
3. I bless the world with light
4. This is my function
5. I am blessed
6. I am at peace

Evening review

(62) Forgiveness is my function as the light of the world

1. My light transcends darkness
2. Forgiveness transcends error
3. I ask my Higher Self to show me what forgiveness is
4. I accept my function
5. I release attack thoughts to the light

"You who are now His means must love all that He loves.
And what you bring is your remembrance of everything that
is eternal."
T–22.VI.6:6-7

My message:

_____

_____

_____

Lesson 82

Morning Review

(63) **The light of the world brings peace to every mind through my forgiveness**

1. I forgive the world that it is healed
2. I forgive my brother that he is healed
3. I forgive myself that I am healed
4. Forgiveness is the light of love
5. The Love of God shines through me

Evening Review

(64) **Let me not forget my function**

1. I remember my light comes from my true Self
2. I willingly release my ego's concern of lack and fear
3. I am light
4. I am love
5. I am joy
6. I am one with all that God created

"Each little gift you offer to your brother lights up the world. Be not concerned with darkness; look away from it and toward your brother. And let the darkness be dispelled by Him Who knows the light, and lays it gently in each quiet smile of faith and confidence with which you bless your brother."

T–22.VI.9:9-11

My Message:

_____

_____

_____

Lesson 83

Morning Review

(65) My only function is the one God gave me

1. I am the light of the world
2. I am here to love
3. I know what I am to do
4. I know what I am to say
5. I am at peace
6. I happily bring peace to the world

Evening Review

(66) My happiness and my function are one

1. I am one with all that God created
2. God created me whole and happy
3. I will not let my will separate me from His
4. I smile with happiness knowing what my function is
5. Thank you God for Your Love
6. Thank you for giving me such a glorious function

"There is a deep responsibility you owe yourself, and one you must learn to remember all the time. The lesson may seem hard at first, but you will learn to love it when you realize that it is true and is but a tribute to your power. You who have sought and found littleness, remember this: Every decision you make stems from what you think you are, and represents the value that you put upon yourself. Believe the little can content you, and by

limiting yourself you will not be satisfied. For your function is not little, and it is only by finding your function and fulfilling it that you can escape from littleness."
T–15.III.3: 1-5

My Message:

_____

_____

_____

Lesson 84

Morning Review

(67) **Love created me like itself**

1. I am in the likeness of my Creator
2. I am not a body
3. I am Love
4. I am light
5. I am forgiveness
6. I am holy

Evening Review

(68) **Love holds no grievances**

1. I release my grievances
2. I will not attack myself or my brother
3. I am the Self God made innocent
4. I am the Self God made in Love
5. Only my Self is real
6. My Self is the light of the world

"The Kingdom is perfectly united and perfectly protected, and the ego will not prevail against it. Amen"
T–4.III.1:12

My Message:

_____

_____

_____

Lesson 85

Morning Review

(69) **My grievances hide the light of the world in me**

1. My grievances are clouds of illusions
2. I willingly release them
3. I let them float away
4. Now does the light behind them shine
5. Now do I transcend to the true vision above the clouds
6. Now I see with the eye of my higher Self

Evening Review

(70) **My salvation comes from me**

1. I am responsible for what I think
2. I can choose to create with Source or with ego
3. I choose to create with Source
4. I choose my healing
5. I choose peace
6. There is no power outside of me that can take my peace

"Could you but realize for a single instant the power of healing that the reflection of God, shining in you, can bring to all the world, you could not wait to make the mirror of your mind clean to receive the image of the holiness that heals the world."
T–14.IX.7:1

My Message:

_____

_____

_____

Lesson 86

Morning Review

(71) Only God's plan for salvation will work

1. God's plan never fails
2. I trust in God
3. I ask Him for guidance
4. I listen with my heart for direction
5. I am willing to step aside
6. I am willing to let God guide

Evening Review

(72) Holding grievances is an attack on God's plan for salvation

1. I release my grievances to God
2. I am cleaning the altar of Self
3. Cleaning the altar, I release guilt
4. I pray to be healed of my misperceptions of myself and my brother
5. We are one
6. We are holy
7. All is well

"If you perceive truly you are cancelling out misperceptions in yourself and in others simultaneously. Because you see them as they are, you offer them your acceptance of their truth so they can accept it for themselves. This is the healing that the miracle induces."

T–3.II.6:5-7

My Message:

_____

_____

_____

Lesson 87

Morning Review

(73) **I will there be light**

1. I will use the power of my will today
2. The will of my Self and the Will of God are one
3. I step aside and let my higher Self guide
4. My Self always guides me in light
5. My Self always guides me in love
6. My Self always guides me in peace
7. Whatever happens today, I will look at it in the light

Evening Review

(74) **There is no will but God's**

1. I am safe
2. I am loved
3. I am whole
4. I am innocent
5. I see all my brother's in the light
6. We are one

"God wills you perfect happiness now. Is it possible that this is not also your will? And is it possible that this is not also the will of your brothers?"
T–9.VII.1:8-10

My Message:

_____

_____

_____

Lesson 88

Morning Review

(75) **The light has come**

1. I choose salvation rather than attack
2. I choose forgiveness rather than grievance
3. I choose innocence rather than guilt
4. I choose oneness rather than separateness
5. I choose light rather than dark
6. I choose happiness rather than despair

Evening Review

(76) **I am under no laws but Gods**

1. I release my beliefs in the laws I made
2. My self-made laws have absolutely no effect on me
3. Only God's laws affect me
4. I am God's perfect creation
5. I am made in perfect Love
6. I am free

"It is still up to you to choose to join with truth or with illusion. But remember that to choose one is to let the other go. Which one you choose you will endow with beauty and reality, because the choice depends on which you value more. The spark of beauty or the veil of ugliness, the real world or the world of guilt and fear, truth or illusion, freedom or slavery – it is all the same. For you can never choose except between God and the ego."

T–17.III.9:1-5

_____

My message:

_____

_____

_____

Lesson 89

Morning Review

(77) I am entitled to miracles

1. I am under no law's but God's
2. Under God's law, miracles occur naturally as expression of Love
3. I am loved
4. I am released from all grievances
5. I release my brothers from all grievances
6. We are holy

Evening Review

(78) Let miracles replace all grievances

1. I unite with my higher Self
2. I am not separate from God, my Self, or my brother
3. I accept my release from guilt
4. I am willingly allow my illusions to be replaced with truth
5. I will have no other truth before me
6. This is the choice I willingly make

"Restore to God His Son as He created him, by teaching him his innocence."

T–14.V. 9:10

My message:

_____

_____

_____

Lesson 90

Morning Review

(79) **Let me recognize the problem so it can be solved**

1. I am willing to see that my problem is some form of grievance that I cherish
2. I am willing to understand that the solution is always a miracle with which I allow the grievance to be replaced
3. The problem is lack of love
4. The solution is love
5. The problem is guilt
6. The solution is innocence

Evening Review

(80) **Let me recognize my problems have been solved**

1. Peace is in every step
2. Love is in every moment
3. God is in every breath
4. This is the solution I bring with me all through the day
5. This is the miracle
6. I need look no further

"If a mind perceives without love, it perceives an empty shell and is unaware of the spirit within. But the Atonement restores spirit to its proper place. The mind that serves spirit is invulnerable." T–1.IV.2:9-11

My message:

_____

_____

_____

Lesson 91

Miracles are seen in the light

1. I am strong
2. I am powerful
3. I am unlimited
4. I am worthy
5. I am God's reality
6. A bridge of light connects me with God
7. In this light, all miracles exist

"If you were one with God and recognized this oneness, you would know His power is yours."
T–22.VI.12:1

Lesson 92

Miracles are seen in light and light and strength are one

1. I see through the light of God
2. I act with the strength of God
3. I think with the Mind of God
4. I accept the truth of who I am
5. I join with my higher Self and we are one
6. I bless all as I am blessed

"Remember that there is no second to Him. There cannot, therefore, be anyone without His Holiness, nor anyone unworthy of His perfect Love. Fail not in your function of loving in a loveless place made out of darkness and deceit, for thus are darkness and deceit undone."
T–14.IV.4:8-10

Lesson 93

Light and joy and peace abide in me

1. I am sinless

2. My sinlessness is guaranteed by God

3. I am as God created me

4. I am one Self

5. Light and joy and peace abide in me

6. In gratitude, I accept this truth

"Child of peace, the light *has* come to you."
T–22.VI.6:1

Lesson 94

I am as God created me

1. I am as God created me

2. I am His Son eternally

3. I stand in strength

4. I stand in light

5. I stand in my one, true Self

6. I am whole

7. I am holy

"You have learned your need of healing. Would you bring anything else to the Sonship, recognizing your need of healing for yourself? For in this lies the beginning of the return to knowledge; the foundation on which God will help build again the thought system you share with Him. Not one stone you place upon it but will be blessed by Him, for you will be restoring the holy dwelling place of His Son, where He wills His Son to be and where he is." T–11.I.1:1-4

Lesson 95

I am one Self, united with my Creator

1. I am light
2. I am peace
3. I am strength
4. I am one Self
5. I am united with my Creator

"Our success in transcending the ego is guaranteed by God, and I share this confidence for both of us and all of us."
T–8.V.4:4

Lesson 96

Salvation comes from my one Self

1. I am my higher, holy, spirit Self

2. I am one with the Mind of God

3. I am peace

4. I am joy

5. I am innocence

6. I allow all else to fall away

"The goal of the curriculum, regardless of the teacher you choose, is 'Know thyself.' There is nothing else to seek."
T–8.III.5:1-2

Lesson 97

I am spirit

1. I am spirit
2. I am a holy child of God
3. I am safe
4. I am healed
5. I am whole
6. I am eternal

"Be humble before Him, and yet great *in* Him. And value no plan of the ego before the plan of God."
T–15.IV.3:1-2

Lesson 98

I will accept my part in God's plan for salvation

1. I accept my part in God's plan for salvation
2. I accept my innocence
3. I accept my God given ability
4. I accept God's peace
5. I accept God's joy
6. I accept God's truth about myself

"Unless the universe were joined in you it would be apart from God, and to be without Him *is* to be without meaning."
T–15.XI.6:6

Lesson 99

Salvation is my only function here

1. Salvation is my only function here
2. It is God's will and so it is mine
3. I forgive myself of all I think I did
4. I keep no secrets from God
5. God's light is in my mind
6. God's love is in my heart
7. We are one

"You who have always loved your Father can have no fear, for any reason, to look within and see your holiness. You cannot be as you believed you were. Your guilt is without reason because it is not in the Mind of God, where you are."
T-13.X.10:5-7

Lesson 100

My part is essential to God's plan for salvation

1. I complete God's plan for salvation
2. I complete God's plan with my happiness
3. I complete God's plan with my joy
4. I complete God's plan with my peace
5. I smile at my Self as we become one
6. My smile saves the world

"There cannot, therefore, be anyone without His Holiness, nor anyone unworthy of His perfect Love. Fail not in your function of loving in a loveless place made out of darkness and deceit, for thus are darkness and deceit undone."
T–14.IV.4:9-10

Lesson 101

God's Will for me is perfect happiness

1. I forgive myself of all I think I did

2. I let the Light of God cleanse my mind

3. I accept that I am the sinless child of God

4. I allow the happiness God wills for me to fill my being

5. I am peace

6. I am whole

7. I am humbled by God's truth of who I am

"There is no question but one you should ever ask of yourself: 'Do I want to know my Father's Will for me?' He will not hide it."
T-8.VI.8:1-2

Lesson 102

I share God's Will for happiness for me

1. I willingly let go of my suffering

2. I willingly let go of my story

3. I willingly accept God's will for me

4. I willingly allow myself to be happy

5. I willingly accept God's Love

6. I stand in gratitude for all I have received

"Behold the great projection, but look on it with the decision that it must be healed, and not with fear. Nothing you made has any power over you unless you still would be apart from your Creator, and with a will opposed to His."
T–22.II.10:1-2

Lesson 103

God being Love, is also happiness

1.   I willingly release my fear of love

2.   I willingly release my fear of God

3.   I willingly accept God's Love

4.   I willingly accept God's happiness

5.   I willingly accept God's Will for me

6.   I willingly accept my Self

7.   I smile at my Self and God smiles back with Love's energy

---

"Think what that instant brought: the recognition that the 'something else' you thought was you is an illusion. And truth came instantly to show you where your Self must be."
T–22.I.10:4-5

Lesson 104

I seek but what belongs to me in truth

1. Within me is God's holy altar

2. I sweep away my illusions and accept His eternal gifts

3. Joy is mine

4. Peace is mine

5. I am one with God

6. My receiving completes His giving

7. I accept God's gifts with deep gratitude

"You are a mirror of truth, in which God Himself shines in perfect light. To the ego's dark glass you need but say, 'I will not look there because I know these images are not true.' Then let the Holy One shine on you in peace knowing that this and only this must be. His Mind shone on you in your creation and brought your mind into being."
T–4.IV.9:1-4

Lesson 105

God's peace and joy are mine

1. I accept God's gift of peace
2. I accept God's gift of joy
3. My accepting God's gifts completes His creation
4. My acceptance completes my Self
5. I accept God's gifts with love and gratitude
6. I extend God's gifts to all

"What is the holy instant but God's appeal to you to recognize what He has given you? Here is the great appeal to reason; the awareness of what is always there to see, the happiness that could be always yours. Here is the constant peace you could experience forever."
T–21.VIII.5:1-3

Lesson 106

Let me be still and listen to the truth

1. I stand in stillness
2. I brush away the ego's voice
3. I am open to truth
4. My Father's Voice calls me and I listen
5. I am His messenger of truth
6. I am His messenger of Love
7. In gratitude I accept my function

"To have faith is to heal. It is the sign that you have accepted the Atonement for yourself, and would therefore share it. By faith, you offer the gift of freedom from the past, which you received."
T–19.I.9:1-2

Lesson 107

Truth will correct all errors in my mind

1. I sweep all illusions from the altar of my mind

2. I am quiet

3. Truth fills my mind

4. I am one with my holy Self

5. I am love

6. I am peace

7. I am whole

"The betrayal of the Son of God lies only in illusion, and all his 'sins' are but his own imagining. His reality is forever sinless. He need not be forgiven but awakened."
T–17.I.1:1-3

Lesson 108

To give and to receive are one in truth

1. My receiving completes God's giving

2. My giving completes my receiving

3. All is one

4. I am one with all truth

5. I am love

6. I am joy

7. I am peace

"The holy instant thus becomes a lesson in how to hold all of your brothers in your mind, experiencing not loss but completion. From this it follows you can only give. And this *is* love, for this alone is natural under the laws of God."
T–15.VI.5:5-7

Lesson 109

I rest in God

1. I rest in God
2. I rest in His light
3. I rest in His peace
4. I rest in His safety
5. I rest in His stillness
6. I rest in the temple He has provided me
7. I open the doors and invite all to join me there
8. Thank you God for this holy renewal

"There are no hidden chambers in God's temple. Its gates are open wide to greet His Son. No one can fail to come where God has called him, if he close not the door himself upon his Father's welcome."

T–14.VI.8:6-8

Lesson 110

I am as God created me

1. I am my higher, holy Self

2. I am eternal

3. I am innocent

4. I am whole

5. I accept this knowing of my Self with love and gratitude

6. I accept that I am as God created me

"How simple is salvation! All it says is what was never true is not true now, and never will be. The impossible has not occurred, and can have no effects. And that is all."
T–31.I.1:1

Review III

Dear one:

We are now starting another review. Please read the directions in the introduction to the review carefully and follow them to the best of your ability. The mirror affirmations may be done in conjunction with the phrases from the review lessons or you may prefer to just do one or the other as your mirror affirmations. As always, follow your own inner guidance in how to do these next reviews.

Lesson 111

Morning Review

(91) **Miracles are seen in the light**

1. I am the light of God
2. I am holy
3. I am innocent

Evening Review

(92) **Miracles are seen in light & light & strength are one**

1. I am the strength of God
2. I accept His gifts
3. I am blessed

"The Atonement can only be accepted within you by releasing the inner light."
T–2.III.1:1

Lesson 112

Morning Review

(93) **Light & joy & peace abide in me**

1. I am the home of light
2. I am the home of joy
3. I am the home of peace
4. I am the home of God

Evening Review

(94) **I am as God created me**

1. God created me as eternal
2. God created me as holy
3. God created me as innocent
4. God and I are one

"Return with me to Heaven, walking together with your brother out of this world and through to another, to the loveliness and joy the other holds within it."
T–18.I.12:4

Lesson 113

Morning Review

(95) **I am one Self, united with my Creator**

1. I am one Self

2. I am whole

3. I am united with my Creator

Evening Review

(96) **Salvation comes from my one Self**

1. I am one Self

2. I am God's innocent child

3. I am whole

"This simple courtesy is all the Holy Spirit asks of you. Let truth be what it is. Do not intrude upon it, do not attack it, do not interrupt its coming. Let it encompass every situation and bring you peace."
T–17.VIII.2:1-4

Lesson 114

Morning Review

(97) I am Spirit

1. I am Spirit
2. I am God's creation
3. I am eternal
4. I am limitless

Evening Review

(98) I will accept my part in God's plan for salvation

1. I accept my function
2. I accept my innocence
3. I receive His gift of peace

"God turns to you to ask the world be saved, for by your own salvation is it healed."
T–30.II.5:1

Lesson 115

Morning Review

(99) Salvation is my only function here

1. I forgive myself
2. I forgive the world
3. We are one
4. We are holy

Evening Review

(100) My part is essential to God's plan for salvation

1. I am essential to God
2. I am essential to the world
3. My part is essential to God's plan for salvation

"It is essential that error be not confused with sin, and it is this distinction that makes salvation possible. For error can be corrected and the wrong made right. But sin, were it possible, would be irreversible."
T-19.II.1:1-3

Lesson 116

Morning Review

(101) God's Will for me is perfect happiness

1. I choose to no longer suffer
2. I am happy
3. I am whole
4. Thank You for Your gift of happiness

Evening Review

(102) I share God's Will for happiness for me

1. I am happy
2. I am complete
3. Thank you for You for Your gift of happiness

"The branch that bears no fruit will be cut off and will wither away. Be glad! The light will shine from the true Foundation of life, and your own thought system will stand corrected."
T-3.VII.6:1-3

Lesson 117

Morning Review

(103) **God being Love is also happiness**

1. God is Love
2. Love is happiness
3. Love brings joy

Evening Review

(104) **I seek what belongs to me in truth**

1. In gratitude I accept God's gift of love
2. In gratitude I accept God's gift of joy
3. My Father and I are one
4. I accept truth

"God wants only His Son because His Son is His only treasure."
T-8.VI.5:1

Lesson 118

Morning Review

(105) **God's peace and joy are mine**

1. I accept God's gift of peace
2. I accept God's gift of joy

Evening Review

(106) **Let me be still and listen to truth**

1. I still my voice and hear only the Voice for truth
2. I am God's perfect child
3. I am loved
4. I am love

"Love, too would set a feast before you, on a table covered with a spotless cloth, set in a quiet garden where no sound but singing and a softly joyous whispering is ever heard. This is a feast that honors your holy relationship, and at which everyone is welcomed as an honored guest."
T-19.IV.i.16:1-2

Lesson 119

Morning Review

(107) **Truth will correct all errors in my mind**

1. I am safe in the Mind of God

2. My Self cannot be hurt

3. I am healed

Evening Review

(108) **To give and to receive are one in truth**

1. I forgive all things

2. I am forgiven of all things

3. I am the sinless child of God

"Only the Thoughts of God are true. And all that follows from them comes from what they are, and is as true as is the holy Source from which they came."
T-17.III.9:7-8

Lesson 120

Morning Review

(109) **I rest in God**

1. I am in quiet
2. I am at peace
3. God and I are sharing love

Evening Review

(110) **I am as God created me.**

1. I am love
2. I am lovable
3. I am holy

"The memory of God comes to the quiet mind. It cannot come where there is conflict, for a mind at war against itself remembers not eternal gentleness."
T-23.I.1:1-2

Lesson 121

Forgiveness is the key to happiness

1. I forgive the self I think I made

2. I forgive the self I think another made

3. I accept giving and receiving are one

4. I accept I am my higher, holy Self

5. My brother and I are one in God

6. We are the holy Son of God

"To you to whom it has been given to save the Son of God from crucifixion and from hell and death, all glory be forever. For you have power to save the Son of God because his father willed that it be so. And in your hands does all salvation lie, to be both offered and received as one."
T- 26.VII.17:4-6

Lesson 122

Forgiveness offers everything I want

1. Today I accept this as true

2. Today I receive the gifts of God

3. Today I am in peace and joy

4. Today I spend in happiness and gratitude

"Forgiveness is the only function meaningful in time."
T-25.VI.5:3

Lesson 123

I thank my Father for His gifts to me

1. I devote today to gratitude

2. I am grateful for God's Love

3. I am grateful for God's blessings

4. I am grateful for my changeless Self

5. I am grateful to be one with God, whole and eternal

"When the Son of God accepts the laws of God as what he gladly wills, it is impossible that he be bound, or limited in any way. In that instant he is as free as God would have him be. For the instant he refuses to be bound, he is not bound."
T-15.VI.5:10-12

Lesson 124

Let me remember I am one with God

1. I re-member my divinity
2. I re-member my true Self
3. I re-member the holy place in my mind
4. God is my Companion as I walk along
5. I am loved
6. We are one

"The Christ in you is very still. He looks on what He loves, and knows it as Himself. And thus does He rejoice at what He sees, because He knows that it is one with Him and with His Father." T-24.V.1:1-3

Lesson 125

In quiet I receive God's Word today

1. I am still

2. I am open only to the voice of God

3. I know I am loved

4. I am sanctified by Him to hear His Word

5. I am sanctified by Him to bring peace to the world

6. All other judgments are meaningless

"And you are asked to let yourself be free of all the dreams of what you never were, and seek no more to substitute the strength of idle wishes for the Will of God."
T-30.IV.7:5

Lesson 126

All that I give is given myself

1. As I give love, I am loved

2. As I give forgiveness, I am forgiven

3. As I give peace, I am peaceful

4. As I give happiness, I am happy

5. As I give my brother innocence, I am innocence

"To have, give all to all."
T-6.V.A. 5:13

Lesson 127

There is no love but God's

1. God is love
2. God is all there is
3. God created all in love
4. I am love
5. All my brothers are love
6. All are equal in God's Love

"When you are afraid, be still and know that God is real, and you are His beloved Son in whom He is well pleased. Do not let your ego dispute this, because the ego cannot know what is as far beyond its reach as you are."
T-4.I.8:6-7

Lesson 128

The world I see holds nothing that I want

1. I willingly let go of all my worldly grievances

2. I willingly let go of all I think I should have done

3. In the present moment I see I have all

4. I am whole

5. I am perfect

6. I seek only God

"In the world of scarcity, love has no meaning and peace is impossible. For gain and loss are both accepted, and so no one is aware that perfect love is in him."
T-15.VI.5:1-2

Lesson 129

Beyond this world there is a world I want

1. I choose a world of peace

2. I choose a world of love

3. I drop the heavy chains I have wrapped around myself

4. I choose to let my higher Self led me into light

5. I remember what I am

6. I am free

7. Thank you

"Yours is the independence of creation, not of autonomy. Your whole creative function lies in your complete dependence on God, Whose function He shares with you."
T-11.V.6:1-2

Lesson 130

It is impossible to see two worlds

1. Only truth is real

2. Only God is real

3. Only love is real

4. I willingly release all that is unreal

5. I rest in God

"The only part of your mind that has reality is the part that links you still with God."
T-14.V.1:1

Lesson 131

No one can fail who seeks to reach the truth

1. Today I walk in faith

2. Today I seek and find all that I want

3. Today I seek only for truth

4. Today I walk with Spirit beside me

5. Today I smile in gratitude and joy

"To justify one value that the world upholds is to deny your Father's sanity and yours. For God and His beloved Son do not think differently."
T-25.VII.4:1-2

Lesson 132

I loose the world from all I thought it was

1. My beliefs create my world

2. My ego is not my creator

3. I am free from my fearful fantasies

4. I am the eternal Self

5. I am one with God

6. I am at peace

"The ego is a wrong minded attempt to perceive yourself as you wish to be rather than as you are. Yet you can know yourself only as you are, because that is all you can be sure of. Everything else *is* open to question."
T-3.IV.2:3-5

Lesson 133

I will not value what is valueless

1. I choose with love not fear
2. I choose what is eternal not immediately satisfying
3. I choose what serves God not ego
4. I choose what brings peace not guilt
5. My hands are empty
6. My mind is open
7. Heaven is my home

"Remember that you always choose between truth and illusion; between the real Atonement that would heal and the ego's 'atonement' that would destroy. The power of God and all His Love, without limit, will support you as you seek only your place in the plan of Atonement arising from His Love."
T-16.VII.10:1-2

Lesson 134

Let me perceive forgiveness as it is

1. As I forgive, I am forgiven

2. As I bless, I am blessed

3. I release the chains that bind me to the world

4. I am free

5. I am innocent

6. I am one with God

"All that is given you is for release; the sight, the vision and the inner Guide all lead you out of hell with those you love beside you, and the universe with them."
T-31.VII.7:7

Lesson 135

If I defend myself I am attacked

1. I am in God's hands
2. I release my fear
3. I release my defenses
4. I am whole
5. I am strong
6. I am healed
7. I am guided to my highest and best good

"Be willing, for an instant, to leave your altars free of what you placed upon them and what is really there you cannot fail to see. The holy instant is not an instant of creation, but of recognition. For recognition comes of vision and suspended judgment."
T-21.II.8:1-3

Lesson 136

Sickness is a defense against the truth

1. I accept the truth of what I am
2. I allow my mind to be wholly healed
3. I release the illusions of my body that I have made
4. I am God's creation not mine
5. I stand in His truth
6. My Self and God are one eternally

"Truth is not frail. Illusions leave it perfectly unmoved and undisturbed."
T-24.III.3:2-3

Lesson 137

When I am healed I am not healed alone

1. I allow my mind to be wholly healed

2. I share my healing with the world

3. I am strong

4. I am free

5. I am one with all there is

6. I am holy

"What God calls one will be forever one, not separate. His Kingdom is united; thus it was created, and thus will it ever be."
T-26.VII.15:7-8

Lesson 138

Heaven is the decision I must make

1. I make the decision for heaven now

2. I make the decision for heaven consciously

3. God goes with me wherever I go

4. God is the strength in which I trust

5. There is nothing to fear

6. I am sustained by the Love of God

7. God is now

"Seek and find His message in the holy instant, where all illusions are forgiven. From there the miracle extends to bless everyone and to resolve all problems."
T-16.VII.11:1-2

Lesson 139

I will accept Atonement for myself

1. I accept Atonement for myself

2. I am as God created me

3. My brothers and sisters are as God created them

4. We are one

5. I walk in love today

6. I walk in gratitude

"You have been told not to make error real, and the way to do this is very simple. If you want to believe in error, you would have to make it real because it is not true. But truth is real in its own right, and to believe in truth *you do not have to do anything.*"
T-12.I.1:1-3

Lesson 140

Only salvation can be said to cure

1. I am the guiltless Son of God

2. My brothers and sisters are the guiltless Son of God

3. We are one

4. I am whole

5. I rest in the mind of God

6. I hear only His Voice

"You need not fear the Higher Court will condemn you. It will merely dismiss the case against you. There can be no case against a child of God, and every witness to guilt in God's creations is bearing false witness to God Himself."
T-5.VI.10:1-3

Review IV

Dear one,

We are at Review IV. Please take the time to read the introduction to the review carefully. The review clearly states: "We add no other thoughts, but let these be the messages they are." (W-Re. IV.In.9:1) Therefore, I was guided not to add any other affirmations to this section.

Lesson 141

My mind holds only what I think with God

(121) Forgiveness is the key to happiness

(122) Forgiveness offers everything I want

"Never approach the holy instant after you have tried to remove all fear and hatred from your mind. That is *its* function. Never attempt to overlook your guilt before you ask the Holy Spirit's help. That is *His* function. Your part is only to offer Him a little willingness to let Him remove all fear and hatred, and to be forgiven."
T-18.V.2:1-5

Lesson 142

My mind holds only what I think with God

(123) I thank my Father for His gifts to me

(124) Let me remember I am one with God

"Guilt makes you blind, for while you see one spot of guilt within you, you will not see the light. And by projecting it the world seems dark, and shrouded in your guilt."
T-13.IX.7:1-2

Lesson 143

My mind holds only what I think with God

(125) **In quiet I receive God's word today**

(126) **All that I give is given to myself**

"Perception rests on choosing; knowledge does not. Knowledge has but one law because it has but one Creator."
T-25.III.3:1-2

Lesson 144

My mind holds only what I think with God

(127) **There is no love but God's**

(128) **The world I see holds nothing that I want**

"When you have let all that obscured the truth in your most holy mind be undone for you, and therefore stand in grace before your Father, He will give Himself to you as He has always done. Giving Himself is all He knows, and so it is all knowledge."
T-14.IV.3:1-2

Lesson 145

My mind holds only what I think with God

(129) Beyond this world there is a world I want

(130) It is impossible to see two worlds

"Glory to God in the highest, and to you because He has so willed it. Ask and it shall be given you, because it has already *been* given. Ask for light and learn that you *are* light. If you want understanding and enlightenment you will learn it, because your decision to learn it is the decision to listen to the Teacher Who knows of light, and can therefore teach it to you."
T-8.III.1:1-4

Lesson 146

My mind holds only what I think with God

(131) **No one can fail who seeks to reach the truth**

(132) **I loose the world from all I thought it was**

"Nothing real can be threatened, nothing unreal exists, herein lies the peace of God."
Preface – Page x

Lesson 147

My mind holds only what I think with God

(133) **I will not value what is valueless**

(134) **Let me perceive forgiveness as it is**

"You do not recognize the enormous waste of energy you expend in denying truth."
T-9.I.11:1

Lesson 148

My mind holds only what I think with God

(135) If I defend myself I am attacked

(136) Sickness is a defense against the truth

"The spark of beauty or the veil of ugliness, the real world or the world of guilt and fear, truth or illusion, freedom or slavery—it is all the same. For you can never choose except between God and the ego."
T.17-III.9:4-5

Lesson 149

My mind holds only what I think with God

(137) **When I am healed I am not healed alone**

(138) **Heaven is the decision I must make**

"There *is* no substitute for love."
T-15.V.6:2

Lesson 150

My mind holds only what I think with God

(139) **I will accept Atonement for myself**

(140) **Only salvation can be said to cure**

"When the light comes and you have said, 'God's Will is mine,' you will see such beauty that you will know it is not of you. Out of your joy you will create beauty in His Name, for your joy could no more be contained than His. The bleak little world will vanish into nothingness, and your heart will be so filled with joy that it will leap into Heaven, and into the Presence of God."
T-11.III.3:3-5

Lesson 151

All things are echoes of the Voice for God

1. I let my thoughts be purified

2. I release to the Holy Spirit the feelings I have made of sadness, guilt, abandonment and unworthiness

3. I accept the healing of my mind

4. I am grateful to know the truth of who I am

5. I am blessed by God

"To deny what is can only *seem* to be fearful. Fear cannot be real without a cause, and God is the only Cause. God is Love and you do want Him. This *is* your will. Ask for this and you will be answered, because you will be asking only for what belongs to you."
T-9.I.9:5-9

Lesson 152

The power of decision is my own

1. I choose God
2. I am that I am
3. I am healed
4. I am whole
5. I am humble
6. I am grateful

"Every situation, properly perceived, becomes an opportunity to heal the Son of God. And he is healed *because* you offered faith to him, giving him to the Holy Spirit and releasing him from every demand your ego would make of him."
T-19.I.2:1-2

Lesson 153

In my defenselessness my safety lies

1. I am defenseless

2. I am safe

3. I am the Son of God

4. God is my strength

5. I am God's messenger

6. I shine His love, strength. and peace to the world

"Teach attack in any form and you have learned it, and it will hurt you. Yet this learning is not immortal, and you can unlearn it by not teaching it."
T-6.III.3:9-10

Lesson 154

I am among the ministers of God

1. I am a minister of God
2. He speaks through my voice
3. My hands hold His messages and carry them to those whom He appoints
4. My feet bring me where He wills me to go
5. My will unites with His
6. I recognize this with humility and gratitude
7. I am free

"The power to work miracles belongs to you. I will provide the opportunities to do them, but you must be ready and willing."
T-1.III.I:7-8

Lesson 155

I will step back and let Him lead the way

1. I walk with Him in peace

2. Our path leads past illusions

3. Our path leads to truth

4. I trust His guidance

5. I am safe

6. I am loved

"Walk in light and do not see the dark companions, for they are not fit companions for the Son of God, who was created *of* light and *in* light. The Great Light always surrounds you and shines out from you."
T-11.III.4:6-7

Lesson 156

I walk with God in perfect holiness

1. My mind is lit with His holiness

2. I light the world with His holiness

3. I light all minds which God created one with me

4. Innocence shines from all creation

5. I know who walks with me

6. God walks with me

"Think of the loveliness that you will see, who walk with Him! And think how beautiful will you and your brother look to the other! How happy you will be to be together, after such a long and lonely journey where you walked alone."
T-22.IV.4:1-3

Lesson 157

Into His Presence would I enter now

1. I remember who I am
2. I remember my holiness
3. I remember I am eternal
4. I remember that I am here to bless
5. I remember I am God's light
6. I remember I walk with God

"Hear, then, the one answer of the Holy Spirit to all the questions the ego raises: You are a child of God, a priceless part of His Kingdom, which He created as part of Him. Nothing else exists and only this is real."
T-6.IV.6:1-2

Lesson 158

Today I learn to give as I receive

1. I am pure mind in Mind
2. I am sinless forever
3. I am created from love
4. I never left my Source
5. This truth is reflected in all I see
6. All is one

"Here is holy ground, in which no substitution can enter, and where only the truth in your brother can abide. Here you are joined in God as much together as you are with Him. The original error has not entered here, nor ever will."
T-18.I.9:3-6

Lesson 159

I give the miracles I have received

1. I am healed
2. I am forgiven
3. I am whole
4. I receive miracles
5. I am the giver of miracles
6. I am love

"There is no order of difficulty in miracles. One is not 'harder' or 'bigger' than another. They are all the same. All expressions of love are maximal."
T-1.I:1-4

Lesson 160

I am at home. Fear is the stranger here

1. I am the Self created by God

2. I am created by His love

3. God and I are joined forever

4. I rest in God

5. Where God is, I am home

"If you are afraid, it is because you saw something that is not there. Yet in that same place you could have looked upon me and all your brothers, in the perfect safety of the Mind which created us. For we are there in the peace of the Father, Who wills to extend His peace through you."
T-12.VII.10:4-6

Lesson 161

Give me your blessing, holy Son of God

1. I love you my brother

2. I thank God for you

3. You are my blessing

4. You are my salvation You are my truth

5. We are one

"A miracle is a service. It is the maximal service you can render to another. It is a way of loving your neighbor as yourself. You recognize your own and your neighbor's worth simultaneously." T-1.I.18:1-4

Lesson 162

I am as God created me

1. I am perfect
2. I am sinless
3. I am whole
4. I am that I am
5. I am holy

"In you is all of Heaven. Every leaf that falls is given life in you. Each bird that ever sang will sing again in you. And every flower that ever bloomed has saved its perfume and its loveliness for you. What aim can supersede the Will of God and of His son that Heaven be restored to him for whom it was created as his only home? Nothing before and nothing after it. No other place; no other state nor time. Nothing beyond nor nearer. Nothing else. In any form."
T-25.IV.5:1-10

Lesson 163

There is no death. The Son of God is free

1. I am eternal

2. I am willingly to release my fear

3. I am held in God's eternal love

4. What God creates cannot die

5. I am not separate from God

6. Thank you, God, for life eternal

7. I am free

"Wholeness heals because it is of the mind. All forms of sickness, even unto death, are physical expressions of the fear of awakening. They are attempts to reinforce sleeping out of fear of waking."
T-8.IX.3:1-3

Lesson 164

Now are we one with Him Who is our Source

1. I am one with Source

2. I can only be in the now

3. I let go of all else and merge with Source

4. I am filled with happiness and love

5. I am at peace

6. I am safe

7. I am holy

"All your striving must be directed against littleness, for it does require vigilance to protect your magnitude in this world. To hold your magnitude in perfect awareness in a world of littleness is a task the little cannot undertake. Yet it is asked of you, in tribute to your magnitude and not your littleness."
T-15.III.4:4-6

Lesson 165

Let not my mind deny the Thought of God

1. The Thought of God created me
2. I am eternal
3. I am one with Source
4. I am filled with happiness and love
5. I am at peace
6. I am safe
7. I am holy

"How can you know whether you chose the stairs to Heaven or the way to hell? Quite easily. How do you feel? Is peace in your awareness? Are you certain which way you go? And are you sure the goal of Heaven can be reached? If not, you walk alone. Ask, then, your Friend to join with you, and give you certainty of where you go."
T-24.II.22:6-13

Lesson 166

I am entrusted with the gifts of God

1. God's trust in me is limitless
2. God's gifts are with me wherever I am
3. I am never alone
4. I am always loved
5. I share God's gifts with the world in love and joy
6. I am abundant

"Here is a feast the Father lays before His Son, and shares it equally with him. And in Their sharing there can be no gap in which abundance falters and grows thin."
T-28.III.9:5-6

Lesson 167

There is one life, and that I share with God

1. God is my Source
2. God is my life
3. God is my holiness
4. God is my perfection
5. God is my Self
6. God and I are eternally one

"What your Father wills of you can never change. The truth in you remains as radiant as a star, as pure as light, as innocent as love itself. And you *are* worthy that your will be done!"
T-31.VI.7:3-5

Lesson 168

Your grace is given me. I claim it now.

1. I am worthy of God's grace
2. I am worthy of God's love
3. I am filled with gratitude
4. I am filled with love for God
5. We stand together in stillness giving and receiving love

"I have spoken before of the higher or 'true' perception, which is so near to truth that God Himself can flow across the little gap." T-5.I.4:9

Lesson 169

By grace I live. By grace I am released.

1. By grace I live

2. By grace I am release

3. By grace I give

4. By grace I will release

5. We are one

6. I accept God's Love

"I give you to the Holy Spirit as part of myself. I know that you will be released, unless I want to use you to imprison myself. In the name of my freedom I choose your release, because I recognize that we will be released together."
T-15.XI.10:5-7

Lesson 170

There is no cruelty in God and none in me

1. I do not fear God
2. God is love
3. I am love
4. My eyes see with love
5. My voice speaks with love
6. I am at peace
7. Love is all there is

"Anger is never justified. Attack has no foundation. It is here escape from fear begins, and will be made complete."
T-30.VI.1:1-3

Review V

Dear one,

It is very important to read the review introduction carefully. For each lesson the mirror work will be (with slight variation) from the introduction:

"God is but Love, and therefore so am I. This Self alone knows Love. This Self alone is perfectly consistent in Its Thoughts: knows Its Creator, understands Itself, is perfect in Its knowledge and Its Love and never changes from Its constant state of union with Its Father and Itself." (W-Re.5.In.4:3-5)

I am repeating these affirmations because as a spiritual counselor, I have found that perhaps the most difficult thing for us to believe is that we are lovable and loved. Therefore, looking in the mirror and seeing ourselves as holy, lovable and one with God cannot be overstated or overdone. You cannot repeat too many times: "God is but Love, and therefore so am I." You are finding your true Self in the mirror. You are the Self of Love!

Lesson 171

God is but Love, and therefore so am I

(151) All Things are echoes of the Voice for God

(152) The power of decision is my own

God is but Love and therefore so am I

1. This Self alone knows Love
2. This Self alone is perfectly consistent in Its Thoughts
3. This Self knows Its Creator
4. This Self is perfect in Its knowledge and Its Love
5. This Self never changes from Its constant state of union with Its Father and Itself

---

"God created His Sons by extending His Thought, and retaining the extensions of His Thought in His Mind."
T-6.II.8:1

Lesson 172

God is but Love, and therefore so am I

(153) In my defenselessness my safety lies

(154) I am among the ministers of God

God is but Love, and therefore so am I

1. This Self alone knows Love
2. This Self alone is perfectly consistent in Its Thoughts
3. This Self knows Its Creator
4. This Self is perfect in Its knowledge and Its Love
5. This Self never changes from Its constant
   state of union with Its Father and Itself

"The Kingdom of Heaven *is* you."
T-4.III.1:4

Lesson 173

God is but Love, and therefore so am I

(155) I will step back and let Him lead the way

(156) I walk with God in perfect holiness

God is but Love, and therefore so am I

1. This Self alone knows Love
2. This Self alone is perfectly consistent in Its Thoughts
3. This Self knows Its Creator
4. This Self is perfect in Its knowledge and Its Love
5. This Self never changes from Its constant
   state of union with Its Father and Itself

___

"Child of peace, the light *has* come to you."
T-22.VI.6:1

___

Lesson 174

God is but Love, and therefore so am I

(157) Into His Presence would I enter now

(158) Today I learn to give as I receive

God is but Love, and therefore so am I

1. This Self alone knows Love
2. This Self alone is perfectly consistent in Its Thoughts
3. This Self knows Its Creator
4. This Self is perfect in Its knowledge and Its Love
5. This Self never changes from Its constant state of union with Its Father and Itself

---

"The graciousness of God will take them gently in, and cover all their sense of pain and loss with the immortal assurance of their Father's Love."
T-14.IX.4:3

Lesson 175

God is but Love, and therefore so am I

(159) I give the miracles I have received

(160) I am at home. Fear is the stranger here

God is but Love, and therefore so am I

1. This Self alone knows Love
2. This Self alone is perfectly consistent in Its Thoughts
3. This Self knows Its Creator
4. This Self is perfect in Its knowledge and Its Love
5. This Self never changes from Its constant state of union with Its Father and Itself

---

"Fear cannot be real without a cause, and God is the only Cause. God is Love and you do want Him."
T-9.I.9:6-7

Lesson 176

God is but Love, and therefore so am I

(161) Give me your blessing, holy Son of God

(162) I am as God created me

God is but Love, and therefore so am I

1. This Self alone knows Love
2. This Self alone is perfectly consistent in Its Thoughts
3. This Self knows Its Creator
4. This Self is perfect in Its knowledge and Its Love
5. This Self never changes from Its constant
   state of union with Its Father and Itself

"Because of your Father's Love you can never forget Him, for no one can forget what God Himself placed in his memory."
T-12.VIII.4:1

Lesson 177

God is but Love, and therefore so am I

(163) There is no death. The Son of God is free

(164) Now are we one with Him Who is our Source

God is but Love, and therefore so am I

1. This Self alone knows Love
2. This Self alone is perfectly consistent in Its Thoughts
3. This Self knows Its Creator
4. This Self is perfect in Its knowledge and Its Love
5. This Self never changes from Its constant
   state of union with Its Father and Itself

"Salvation seeks to prove there is no death, and only life exists."
T-29.VII.10:2

Lesson 178

God is but Love, and therefore so am I

(165) Let not my mind deny the Thought of God

(166) I am entrusted with the gifts of God

God is but Love, and therefore so am I

1. This Self alone knows Love
2. This Self alone is perfectly consistent in Its Thoughts
3. This Self knows Its Creator
4. This Self is perfect in Its knowledge and Its Love
5. This Self never changes from Its constant state of union with Its Father and Itself

---

"Sharing is God's way of creating, and also yours."
T-3.IV.3:3

Lesson 179

God is but Love, and therefore so am I

(167) There is one Life, and that I share with God

(168) Your grace is given me. I claim it now

God is but Love, and therefore so am I

1. This Self alone knows Love
2. This Self alone is perfectly consistent in Its Thoughts
3. This Self knows Its Creator
4. This Self is perfect in Its knowledge and Its Love
5. This Self never changes from Its constant state of union with Its Father and Itself

---

"Ask and it shall be given you, because it has already *been* given."
T-8.III.1:2

Lesson 180

God is but Love, and therefore so am I

(169) By grace I live. By grace I am released.

(170) There is no cruelty in God and none in me

God is but Love, and therefore so am I

1. This Self alone knows Love
2. This Self alone is perfectly consistent in Its Thoughts
3. This Self knows Its Creator
4. This Self is perfect in Its knowledge and Its Love
5. This Self never changes from Its constant state of union with Its Father and Itself

---

"Offer your brother freedom and complete release from sin, here in the garden of seeming agony and death."
T-19.IV.D.18:4

Dear one, be sure and read the introduction to lessons 181-200

Lesson 181

I trust my brothers who are one with me

1. I trust my brothers innocence
2. I trust my brothers holiness
3. I trust that we are one
4. I focus on his sinlessness
5. I find my Self in him
6. I see only in the present moment

"See him through the Holy Spirit in his mind, and you will recognize Him in yours. What you acknowledge in your brother you are acknowledging in yourself, and what you share you strengthen."
T-5.III.3:4-5

Lesson 182

I will be still an instant and go home

1. I welcome you my Child, my Self

2. I let all else go to be with You awhile

3. Together, we are in peace

4. Together, we are in love

5. All thoughts of the world fall away and there is just us; my Child, my innocence, my higher, holy Self

6. I am grateful for my Child's remembrance of all that is pure and holy

7. Thank you, I love You

"What is a miracle but this remembering? And who is there in whom this memory lies not? The light in one awakens it in all."
T-21. I.10:4-6

Lesson 183

I call upon God's Name and on my own

1. I am that I am

2. I am holy

3. I am the Self that is one with God

4. I receive God's miracles and I give them to the world

5. I call upon God's name and all else falls away

6. I call upon God's name and I find eternal peace

"God is with you, my brother. Let us join in Him in peace and gratitude, and accept His gift as our most holy and perfect reality, which we share in Him."
T-18.I.10:8-9

Lesson 184

The Name of God is my inheritance

1. I am God energy
2. I have never split from my Source
3. All is united in God energy
4. All is one
5. My spiritual vision sees only wholeness
6. I am that I am
7. I am blessed

"By accepting the Atonement for yourself, you are deciding against the belief that you can be alone, thus dispelling the idea of separation and affirming your true identification with the whole Kingdom as literally part of you."
T-7.VIII.7:3

Lesson 185

I want the peace of God

1. I want only peace
2. I willing surrender my dream world
3. I will not compromise
4. I see that all dreams are one
5. I choose God's peace
6. I share the gift of peace with all the world

"This year determine not to deny what has been given you by God. Awake and share it, for that is the only reason He has called to you. His Voice has spoken clearly, and yet you have so little faith in what you heard, because you have preferred to place still greater faith in the disaster you have made. Today let us resolve together to accept the joyful tidings that disaster is not real and that reality is not disaster."
T-16.II.8:2-5

Lesson 186

Salvation of the world depends on me

1. My function is to fulfill the part God has given me in the salvation of the world

2. I accept my function with true humility

3. God's voice will direct me in what to do and what to say

4. I trust in God's evaluation of my worthiness

5. I do not let my ego's arrogance stop me

6. I dive below the shifting emotions of my mind

7. I am the changeless Son of God

"*You* know what your Creator wills is possible, but what you made believes it is not so. Now must you choose between yourself and an illusion of yourself. Not both, but one."
T-22.II.6:5-7

Lesson 187

I bless the world because I bless myself

1. I have therefore I give

2. My giving strengthens my having

3. On my holy altar are all the blessings I have given and all the blessings I have received

4. These blessings are eternal

5. I am one with God, the Creator, the one Source

6. I am one Self with my brothers

7. We are the one Son of God

"Seek and *find* His message in the holy instant, where all illusions are forgiven. From there the miracle extends to bless everyone and to resolve all problems, be they perceived as great or small, possible or impossible. There is nothing that will not give place to Him and to His Majesty."
T-16.VII.11:1-3

Lesson 188

The peace of God is shining in me now

1. God's light is in me now

2. I am enlightened

3. My true Self carries the eternal light given me by Source

4. My light of peace and love extends from my heart and goes around the world

5. My light blesses all living things as it comes back and blesses me

6. Inwardly I see this circle of peace and love

7. God is thankful to me for extending it and I am thankful to Him for giving it

---

"You have been wrong in thinking that it is needful to prepare yourself for Him. It is impossible to make arrogant preparations for holiness, and not believe that it is up to you to establish the conditions for peace. God has established them."
T-18.IV.4:3-5

Lesson 189

I feel the Love of God within me now

1. God's light is in me now

2. God's light shows me a world of love,
   peace, hope and innocence

3. With God's light shining in me, I bring the
   world blessing and forgiveness

4. The world reflects that which I feel within

5. My heart is quiet and my mind is open

6. In stillness, God finds His way to me

"The light expands and covers everything, extending to infinity
forever shining and with no break or limit anywhere. Within it
everything is joined in perfect continuity. Nor is it possible to
imagine that anything could be outside, for there is nowhere that
this light is not."
T-21.I.8:4-6

Lesson 190

I choose the joy of God instead of pain

1. I willingly surrender the cruel sword of judgment that I hold against my throat

2. I choose joy

3. I choose holiness

4. I choose the peace of God

5. I choose the light of heaven

"There is no pain, no trial, no fear that teaching this can fail to overcome. The power of God Himself supports this teaching, and guarantees its limitless results."
T-14.V.6:-7

Lesson 191

I am the holy Son of God Himself

1. God's Son is my true Identity
2. I am as God created me
3. In recognition of my true Identity, I save the world
4. In recognition of my true Identity, I bless the world
5. In recognition of my true Identity, I bring peace and love to all
6. I am the holy Son of God Himself

"Yet this a vision is which you must share with everyone you see, for otherwise you will behold it not. To give this gift is how to make it yours. And God ordained, in loving kindness, that it be for you."
T-31.VIII.8:5-7

Lesson 192

I have a function God would have me fill

1. I accept that my Self is the sacred Son of God

2. I accept that God created my Self to complete Himself

3. I accept that my Self was created from
   God's Love and is eternal

4. I accept that each of my brothers was created in this same way

5. I accept that through forgiveness I see our holiness

6. I accept these truths with humility and with gratitude

"Dream of your brother's kindnesses instead of dwelling in your dreams on his mistakes. Select his thoughtfulness to dream about instead of counting up the hurts he gave. Forgive him his illusions, and give thanks to him for all the helpfulness he gave." T-27.VII.15:3-5

Lesson 193

All things are lessons God would have me learn

1. Forgive and I will see this differently
2. Forgiveness is the end of my guilt
3. Forgiveness is the end of my fear
4. Forgiveness is the salvation of the world
5. Forgiveness is where my power lies

"All uncertainty comes from the belief that you are under the coercion of judgment. You do not need judgment to organize your life, and you certainly do not need it to organize yourself. In the presence of knowledge all judgment is automatically suspended, and this is the process that enables recognition to replace perception."
T-3.VI.3:4-6

Lesson 194

I place the future in the Hands of God

1. I release the future

2. I place all "time" in the loving Hands of God where all is one

3. Now is each instant a holy instant

4. In each holy instant is my freedom

5. In each holy instant is the world's freedom

6. With one symbolic gesture, I place all my unhealed perceptions from my small hand to God's loving Hands

7. He replaces them with joy and peace

"The Thought of God surrounds your little kingdom, waiting at the barrier you built to come inside and shine upon the barren ground. See how life springs up everywhere."
T-18.VIII.9:1-2

Lesson 195

Love is the way I walk in gratitude

1. I walk in gratitude

2. My gratitude is expressed with love

3. I am joined with every living thing

4. I forgive without comparing

5. When an unhealed thought comes into my mind, I replace it with gratitude

6. I am humbled by the gifts and love God gives me

7. All I need say to God and all living things is: "Thank you. I love you."

"How beautiful it is to walk clean and redeemed and happy, through a world in bitter need of the redemption that your innocence bestows upon it! What can you value more than this? For here is your salvation and your freedom."
T-23.In.6:5-7

Lesson 196

It can be but myself I crucify

1. My brothers safety is my own

2. In my brothers healing I am healed

3. I am not an ego filled with fear

4. I am the beloved Son of God

5. I am strong

6. I am free

7. I but remember that in my defenselessness my safety lies

"You have the right to all the universe; to perfect peace, complete deliverance from all effects of sin, and to the life eternal, joyous and complete in every way, as God appointed for His holy Son."
T-25.VIII.14:1

Lesson 197

It can be but my gratitude I earn

1. I release my conditioned illusion that I must receive gratitude from my brother for my gifts of love and forgiveness

2. I will not let myself combine God's gifts with worldly guilt

3. All gifts I give I received from God

4. I am grateful to Him that I have these gifts to give

5. I give these gifts in gratitude to God and to the one Self of all my brothers

6. God and my Self give eternal gratitude for the gifts I share

---

"What hatred has released to love becomes the brightest light in Heaven's radiance. And all the lights in Heaven brighter grow, in gratitude for what has been restored."
T-26.IX.6:5-6

Lesson 198

Only my condemnation injuries me

1. My illusions make illusion
2. Forgiveness is the only illusion that will erase the rest
3. I free myself when I forgive
4. In forgiveness I merge with my true Self
5. I am one with God
6. I am at peace

"You are a mirror of truth, in which God Himself shines in perfect light. To the ego's dark glass you need but say, 'I will not look there because I know these images are not true.' Then let the Holy One shine on you in peace knowing that this and only this must be."

T-4.IV.9:1-3

Lesson 199

I am not a body I am free

1. I am unlimited

2. I am not bound to space or time

3. I am free

4. My mind rests in God, the Source of Love

5. I am innocent

6. I am immortal

7. My body is a vehicle to bring love and forgiveness wherever the Source of Love sends me

---

"No one believes there really was a time when he knew nothing of a body, and could never have conceived this world as real. He would have seen at once that these ideas are one illusion, too ridiculous for anything but to be laughed away."
T-27.VIII.5:5-6

Lesson 200

There is no peace accept the peace of God

1. I repeat this in gratitude

2. I repeat this in freedom

3. I repeat this in joy

4. I repeat this in union with all my brothers

5. I repeat this to free the world

"The only way to have peace is to teach peace. By teaching peace you must learn it yourself, because you cannot teach what you still dissociate."
T-6.III.4:3-4

<u>Review VI</u>

Dear one,

Read the introduction to the review very carefully before beginning. As stated in the review, we will start each review with: "I am not a body. I am free. For I am still as God created me." When an unwanted thought comes into the mind say: "This thought I do not want. I choose instead…" and repeat the idea for the day. Be gentle with this, it is not an attack on the ego, but a willingness to watch it and let go of its mindless chatter.

Lesson 201

I am not a body. I am free.
For I am still as God created me.

(181) I trust my brothers who are one with me.

1. No one but is my brother

2. I am blessed with oneness with the universe and God

3. My Self is forever One with all that is

"To you and your brother, in whose special relationship the Holy Spirit entered, it is given to release and be released from the dedication to death."
T-29.IV.C.1:1

Lesson 202

I am not a body. I am free.
For I am still as God created me.

(182) I will be still an instant and go home.

1.   I will not choose to stay an instant more where I do not belong

2.   God Himself has given me His Voice to call me home

"Yet the Holy Spirit remembers it for you, and He will guide you to your home because that is His mission."
T-12.IV.5:5

Lesson 203

I am not a body. I am free.
For I am still as God created me.

(183) **I call upon God's Name and on my own.**

1. The Name of God is my deliverance from every thought of evil

2. The Name of God is my deliverance from every thought of sin

3. The Name of God is my own as well as His

"Seek not outside yourself. For it will fail, and you will weep each time an idol falls."
T-29.VII.1:1

Lesson 204

I am not a body. I am free.
For I am still as God created me.

(184) The Name of God is my inheritance.

1. God's Name reminds me that I am His Son
2. I am not a slave to time
3. I am not bound by laws which rule the world of sick illusions
4. I am free
5. I am one with Him

"This course will teach you only what is now. A dreadful instant in a distant past, now perfectly corrected, is of no concern nor value."
T-26.V.10:2-3

Lesson 205

I am not a body. I am free.
For I am still as God created me.

(185) I want the peace of God.

1. The peace of God is everything I want

2. The peace of God is my one goal

3. The peace of God is the aim of my living here

4. The peace of God is my purpose here

5. The peace of God is my function here

"Abide in peace, where God would have you be."
T-26.VII.19:1

Lesson 206

I am not a body. I am free.
For I am still as God created me.

(186) Salvation of the world depends on me.

1. I am entrusted with the gifts of God
2. I am His Son
3. I give His gifts where He intended them to be
4. I bless the world

"God turns to you to ask the world be saved, for by your own salvation is it healed."
T-30.II.5:1

Lesson 207

I am not a body. I am free.
For I am still as God created me.

(187) I bless the world because I bless myself

1. God abides in me

2. His blessing shines upon me from within my heart

3. I turn to Him and every sorrow melts away

4. I accept His boundless Love for me

"Behold your role within the universe! To every part of true creation has the Lord of Love and life entrusted all salvation from the misery of hell. And to each one has He allowed the grace to be a savior to the holy ones especially entrusted to his care."
T-31.VII.8:1-3

Lesson 208

I am not a body. I am free.
For I am still as God created me.

(188) The peace of God is shining in me now

1. I will be still

2. let the earth be still along with me

3. In that stillness we will find the peace of God

4. The peace of God is within my heart

5. My heart witnesses to God Himself

"Health is inner peace. It enables you to remain unshaken by lack of love from without and capable, through your acceptance of miracles, of correcting the conditions proceeding from lack of love in others."
T-2.I.5:11-12

Lesson 209

I am not a body. I am free.
For I am still as God created me.

(189) I feel the Love of God within me now

1. The Love of God is what created me

2. The Love of God is everything I am

3. The Love of God proclaimed me as His Son

4. The Love of God within me sets me free

"Everything meets in God, because everything was created by Him and in Him."
T-6.II.7:6

Lesson 210

I am not a body. I am free.
For I am still as God created me.

(190) **I choose the joy if God instead of pain.**

1. Pain is my own idea

2. Pain is not God's Will

3. I choose His Will, not my own

4. God's Will is joy

5. I choose joy

"As always, your choice is determined by what you value."
T-10.V.14:7

Lesson 211

I am not a body. I am free.
For I am still as God created me.

(191) I am the holy Son of God Himself.

1. I seek God's glory in silence

2. I seek God's glory in true humility

3. I am the Son He created as my Self

4. I am holy

5. I am blessed

"Hear, then, the one answer of the Holy Spirit to all the questions the ego raises: You are a child of God, a priceless part of His Kingdom, which He created as part of Him. Nothing else exists and only this is real."
T-6.IV.6:1-2

Lesson 212

I am not a body. I am free.
For I am still as God created me.

(192) I have a function God would have me fill.

1. I seek the function that sets me free from
   all the illusions of the world

2. Only the function God has given me can offer freedom

3. Only this I seek

4. Only this will I accept as mine

"As your function in Heaven is creation, so your function on earth
is healing."
T-12.VII.4:7

Lesson 213

I am not a body. I am free.
For I am still as God created me.

(193) **All things are lessons God would have me learn**

1. A lesson is a miracle which God offers to me

2. I replace the thoughts I made with God's miracle

3. My thoughts imprison me

4. Through His teaching, I am set free

5. I choose to learn His lessons and forget my own

"Miracles are examples of right thinking, aligning your
perceptions with truth as God created it."
T-I.I.36:1

Lesson 214

I am not a body. I am free.
For I am still as God created me.

(194) I place the future in the hands of God

1. The past is gone
2. The future is not yet
3. I am freed from both
4. What God gives can only be for good
5. I accept what He gives
6. What God gives belongs to me

"What waits in perfect certainty beyond salvation is not our concern."
T-28.III.1:1

Lesson 215

I am not a body. I am free.
For I am still as God created me.

(195) Love is the way I walk in gratitude.

1. The Holy Spirit is my only Guide

2. He walks with me in love

3. I give thanks to Him for showing me the way

4. I remember to walk in love

"Bringing illusion to truth, or the ego to God, is the Holy Spirit's only function."
T-14.IX.1:4

Lesson 216

I am not a body. I am free.
For I am still as God created me.

(196) It can be but myself I crucify.

1. All that I do I do unto myself
2. If I attack, I suffer
3. If I forgive, salvation will be given me
4. I choose to forgive
5. I choose to love

"Love is your power, which the ego must deny. It must also deny everything this power gives you *because* it gives you everything."
T-7.VI.4:7-8

Lesson 217

I am not a body. I am free.
For I am still as God created me.

(197) It can be but my gratitude I earn

1. I am grateful for my salvation

2. I am grateful that through salvation I find my true Self

3. My true Self is free

4. My true Self offers me my eternal innocence

5. I thank my true Self for all its gift

"Rest in His Love and protect your rest by loving. But love everything He created, of which you are a part, or you cannot learn of His peace and accept His gift for yourself and as yourself."
T-7.VII.6:4-6

Lesson 218

I am not a body. I am free
For I am still as God created me.

(198) Only my condemnation injures me

1. My condemnation keeps my vision dark
2. My condemnation keeps me from seeing the vision of my glory
3. I release my condemnation
4. I behold my glory and I am glad
5. I behold my glory and I am thankful

"Do not defend this senseless dream, in which God is bereft of what He loves, and you remain beyond salvation."
T-24.IV.5:1

Lesson 219

I am not a body. I am free.
For I am still as God created me.

(199) I am not a body. I am free

1. I am God's Son

2. Let there be no confusion in me on this truth

3. I am loved forever as God's Son

4. I am His holy child

"The exaltation of the body is given up in favor of the spirit, which you love as you could never love the body. And the appeal of death is lost forever as Love's attraction stirs and calls you. From beyond each of the obstacles to love, Love Itself has called."
T-19.IV.D.5:4-6

Lesson 220

I am not a body. I am free.
For I am still as God created me.

(200) There is no peace except the peace of God

1. Peace is the only way

2. His way is the way of peace

3. His way is the way of love

"The Thought of God surrounds your little kingdom, waiting at the barrier you built to come inside and shine upon the barren ground. See how life springs up everywhere! The desert becomes a garden, green and deep and quiet, offering rest to those who lost their way and wander in the dust."
T-18.VIII.9:1-3

Dear one,

We have reached the end of Part I of the workbook. We will now begin Part II. Before you move on, take a moment and acknowledge yourself for the commitment you have made that has led you this far and the willingness you have shown to release thoughts of fear and unworthiness. Even if you still have ego chatter (which I will tell you that I certainly do), I assure you that you have come much further than you realize. Some of us may never be able to get rid of the ego chatter, but to be aware of it and gently release it is a major step in awakening.

Before you begin Part II of the workbook, it is of utmost importance that you carefully read the introduction.

Dear one, read #1: "What is Forgiveness?"

Lesson 221

Peace to my mind. Let all my thoughts be still

1. I am silent
2. I wait for the Voice of God with all my heart and Soul
3. I wait with my elder brother
4. I have confidence as our minds are joined
5. I seek only the peace of God and His gentle guidance

"And turn you to the stately calm within, where in holy stillness dwells the living God you never left, and Who never left you. The Holy Spirit takes you gently by the hand, and retraces with you your mad journey outside yourself, leading you gently back to the truth and safety within."
T-18.I.8:2-3

Lesson 222

God is with me. I live and move in Him

1. God is my Source of life
2. All that sustains me comes through God
3. His Love surrounds and protects me
4. His thoughts always guide me
5. God is my home
6. I rest in His Love

"It is His Will you share His Love for you, and look upon yourself as lovingly as He conceived of you before the world began, and as He knows you still. God changes not His Mind about His Son with passing circumstance which has no meaning in eternity where He abides, and you with Him."
T-24.VI.3:4-5

Lesson 223

God is my life, I have no life but His

1. I am one with God

2. In God is my real home

3. In God are my real thoughts

4. In God is the Spirit which directs me

5. In God, the great I Am, is all that I am

"Brother, the war against yourself is almost over. The journey's end is at the place of peace. Would you not now accept the peace offered you here?"
T-23.I.4:1-3

Lesson 224

God is my Father and He loves His Son

1. I am innocent
2. I am guiltless
3. I am the light of the world
4. In gratitude and joy I share my gift from God with all the world
5. This is the only reality there is
6. I rejoice in knowing my true Identity and my brother's

"For holiness is seen through holy eyes that look upon the innocence within, and thus expect to see it everywhere. And so they call it forth in everyone they look upon, that he may be what they expect of him."
T-31.VII.11:3-4

Lesson 225

God is my Father, and His Son loves Him

1. I stretch my hand to my Father

2. His hand reaches back to me

3. We are one

4. We share a love that is eternal

5. With love in my heart and a smile on my face, I spend my days in His presence

6. Here is peace found

"Could any part of God be without His Love, and could any part of His Love be contained? God is your heritage, because His one gift is Himself."
T-11.I.7:1-2

Lesson 226

My home awaits me. I will hasten there

1. I have changed my mind about the purpose of the world

2. I am here to bring love

3. I am here to bring forgiveness

4. I am here to bring joy

5. I am relieved to let go of the false and realize the truth

---

"To use the power God has given you as He would have it used is natural. It is not arrogant to be as He created you, nor to make use of what He gave to answer all His Son's mistakes and set him free. But it is arrogant to lay aside the power that He gave, and choose a little senseless wish instead of what He wills."
T-26.VII.18:1-3

Lesson 227

This is my holy instant of release

1. I am free
2. I release all my illusions about the tiny reality I think I made
3. I accept the truth of God in its place
4. This is my holy instant of release
5. Father, I know my will is one with Yours
6. I am home

"The Thought God holds of you is perfectly unchanged by your forgetting. It will always be exactly as it was before the time when you forgot, and will be just the same when you remember."
T-30.III.7:6-7

Lesson 228

God has condemned me not. No more do I

1. My Father knows my holiness

2. It is arrogant of me to think I know better than He does

3. It is arrogant of me to replace my truth in place of His Truth

4. I release my dreams of failure and unworthiness

5. I humbly and gratefully accept the holiness my Father bestowed upon me as part of His creation

6. Thank You

7. I love You

"To accept yourself as God created you cannot be arrogance, because it is the denial of arrogance. To accept your littleness is arrogant, because it means that you believe your evaluation of yourself is truer than God's."
T-9.VIII.10:8-9

Lesson 229

Love, which created me, is what I am

1. My Identity is holy

2. I am love

3. I am sinless

4. I am one with the eternal I Am

5. I am home

6. I am thankful

"A dream of judgment came into the mind that God created perfect as Himself. And in that dream was Heaven changed to hell, and God made enemy unto His Son."
T-29.IX.2:1-2

Lesson 230

Now will I seek and find the peace of God

1. I was created in peace

2. My peaceful Self is unchanged

3. My peaceful Self is eternal

4. This is the truth of who I am

5. Thank you God that what you created is forever true

"The miracle but calls your ancient Name, which you will recognize because the truth is in your memory."
T-26.VII.16:1

Dear one, read #2: "What Is Salvation?"

Lesson 231

Father I will but to remember you

1. I will only for your Love
2. I release all my other meaningless desires
3. Your Love is beyond anything this world can offer
4. You Love is my salvation
5. Thank you for your eternal Love

"You do not want the world. The only thing of value in it is whatever part of it you look upon with love. This gives it the only reality it will ever have."
T-12.VI.3:1-2

Lesson 232

Be in my mind, my Father, through the day

1. I invite my dear Father to be in my mind through the day

2. I clean out all illusions to make room for Him

3. He is my divine Guest

4. I am humble and grateful that He is dwelling within me

5. I am safe

6. I am at peace

"The Thoughts of God are far beyond all change, and shine forever. They await not birth. They wait for welcome and remembering."
T-30.III.8:1-3

Lesson 233

I give my life to God to guide today

1. God is my Guide today

2. I am led by Him

3. When my own thoughts intrude on His guidance, I lay them down

4. He purifies my mind

5. I step aside

6. I let Him Guide

7. Thank you, God, for your gifts

"That is why you must choose to hear one of two voices within you. One you made yourself, and that one is not of God. But the other is given you by God, Who asks you only to listen to it."
T-5.II.3:4-6

Lesson 234

Father, today I am Your Son again

1. Today is my salvation

2. Today I know I am innocent

3. Today I know I am loved

4. Today I know I am safe

5. Today I know I am one with God

6. I walk in gratitude for these eternal truths

"Not one light in Heaven but goes with you. Not one Ray that shines forever in the Mind of God but shines on you. Heaven is joined with you to give the little spark of your desire the power of God Himself, can you remain in darkness?"
T-18.III.8:1-3

Lesson 235

God in His mercy wills that I be saved

1. God's will for me is only happiness

2. God's will is that I be saved from all that hurts me

3. God's love always surrounds me

4. I don't know what anything is for

5. I am the holy child of God

"The meaning of the Son of God lies solely in his relationship with his Creator. If it were elsewhere it would rest on contingency, but there *is* nothing else. And this is wholly loving and forever."
T-20.VI.1:1-3

Lesson 236

I rule my mind, which I alone must rule

1. I alone direct my mind to truth or illusion

2. I alone direct my mind to love or fear

3. I alone direct my mind to serve my ego or the Divine

4. Today, I give my mind to the Divine

5. I listen only to Its direction

"Consider how much vigilance you have been willing to exert to protect your ego, and how little to protect your right mind. Who but the insane would undertake to believe what is not true, and then protect this belief at the cost of truth?"
T-4.III.10:3-4

Lesson 237

Now would I be as God created me

1. Today I will accept the truth about myself
2. Today I will allow the light in me to shine upon the world
3. Today I bring light to the world to end the darkness
4. Today I am one with my divine Self and all my brothers
5. Thank you, God, for Your eternal truth

"His Mind shone on you in your creation and brought your mind into being. His Mind still shines on you and must shine through you."
T-4.IV.9:4-6

Lesson 238

On my decision all salvation rests

1. I am worthy of my Father's trust

2. I am beloved by my Father

3. He assures me of my holiness

4. He entrusts me with His Son's salvation as my Self

5. I am in gratitude of all my Father has given to me

"It is given you to learn how to deny insanity, and come forth from your private world in peace. You will see all that you denied in your brothers because you denied it in yourself. For you will love them, and by drawing nigh unto them you will draw them to yourself, perceiving them as witnesses to the reality you share with God."

T13.V.7:7-9

Lesson 239

The glory of my Father is my own

1. I will not let the truth about myself be hidden by false humility

2. I will not let the truth about myself be hidden by thoughts of unworthiness

3. I will not let the truth about myself be hidden by thoughts of guilt

4. I am thankful for God's gifts

5. I accept His glory and share it with all my brothers

6. This is my salvation

7. Herein lies the peace of all creation

"Everyone in the world must play his part in its redemption, in-order to recognize that the world has been redeemed."
T-12.VII.2:1

Lesson 240

Fear is not justified in any form

1. I will not deceive myself with fearful thoughts
2. I will not let fear steal from me the peace of God
3. I will not let fear steal the truth of God
4. I am God's holy child
5. I am one with all my brothers in love

"For truth *is* true. What else could ever be, or ever was? This simple lesson holds the key to the dark door that you believe is locked forever."
T-14.II.7:3-6

Dear one, read #3: "What Is the World?"

Lesson 241

The holy instant is salvation come

1. Today is a day of joy

2. Today is a day of celebration

3. Today is the world set free

4. Today I forgive the world as I am forgiven

5. I am home

6. All is one

"How long is an instant? As long as it takes to re-establish perfect sanity, perfect peace and perfect love for everyone, for God and for yourself."
T-15.I.14:1-2

Lesson 242

This day is God's. It is my gift to Him

1. I will not lead my life alone today

2. I ask the Holy Spirit within to lead me

3. I am open and willing to listen

4. I come with no desire but to find God

5. I come with gratitude and love that in my willingness it is done

---

"Rest in His Love and protect your rest by loving. But love everything He created, of which you are a part, or you cannot learn of His peace and accept His gift for yourself and as yourself."
T-7.VII.6:4-6

Lesson 243

Today I will judge nothing that occurs.

1. In humility I see my limited knowing
2. I accept that I do not know the whole by piecing together the fragments of my perception
3. I accept I am not capable of judging anything
4. It is a relief to know that this is so
5. I am free
6. I am at peace

"There is a tendency to fragment, and then to be concerned about the truth of just a little part of the whole. And this is but a way of avoiding, or looking away from the whole, to what you think you might be better able to understand. For this is but another way in which you would still try to keep understanding to yourself."
T-16.II.2:1-3

Lesson 244

I am in danger nowhere in the world

1. I am held in my Father's arms

2. I call His name and I am safe

3. I am enfolded by His Love eternally

4. I am secure

5. I am home

"To be alone is to be separated from infinity, but how can this be if infinity has no end? No one can be beyond the limitless, because what has no limits must be everywhere."
T-11.I.2:1-2

Lesson 245

Your peace is with me Father, I am safe

1. God's peace surrounds me wherever I go
2. God's peace shines from my heart to
   the world like a miner's lantern
3. Send Your Sons to me dear God, that I might light their way
4. Send Your Sons to me dear God, that we may heal together
5. Send Your Sons to me, that I may recognize my Self

"The peace of God is given you with the glowing purpose in which you join with your brother. The holy light that brought you and him together must extend, as you accept it."
T-18.I.13:5-6

Lesson 246

To love my Father is to love His Son

1. The path to God is love
2. With love I recognize God in all my brothers
3. With love I find my Self
4. With love I join with God and feel His Love surround me
5. Thank you, thank you – I am loved

"Behold your role within the universe! To every part of true creation has the Lord of Love and life entrusted all salvation from misery of hell. And to each one has He allowed the grace to be a savior to the holy ones especially entrusted to his care."
T-31.VII.8:1-3

Lesson 247

Without Forgiveness I will still be blind

1. Through forgiveness I see the Divine in all I behold

2. It is with this holy light that I am healed

3. I look on my brother with this holy sight and
   see his beauty reflecting back my own

4. We both stand forgiven

5. In this way do I honor God

6. In this way do I show Him my love

"The innocent release in gratitude for their release. And what
they see upholds their freedom from imprisonment and death.
Open your mind to change, and there will be no ancient penalty
exacted from your brother or yourself."
T-31.III.7:1-3

Lesson 248

Whatever suffers is not part of me

1. I own God's Truth
2. I disown my self-made self-concepts and deceits
3. I see them for the lies they are
4. I am holy
5. All God's Sons are holy
6. We are one

"Every dark lesson that you bring to Him Who teaches light He will accept from you, because you do not want it. And He will gladly exchange each one for the bright lesson He has learned for you. Never believe that any lesson you have learned apart from Him means anything."
T-14.XI.4:7-9

Lesson 249

Forgiveness ends all suffering and loss

1. In forgiveness is my suffering over
2. In forgiveness do I cleanse the world of all darkness leaving only the glowing light of love
3. In forgiveness I find joy and abundance
4. In forgiveness I am charitable and giving
5. In forgiveness is what I wish the world to reflect back to me
6. In forgiveness is my holy, loving mind returned to me

"Ask not to be forgiven, for this has already been accomplished. Ask, rather, to learn how to forgive, and to restore what always was to your unforgiving mind. Atonement becomes real and visible to those who use it. On earth this is your only function and you must learn that it is all you want to learn."
T-14.IV.3:4-5

Lesson 250

Let me not see myself as limited

1. Today I see the Son of God

2. Today I behold his holiness

3. Today I wipe illusion from my eyes and see the Truth of my brother who is my Self

4. Today do I know we are one in God

"Decide that God is right and you are wrong about yourself. He created you out of Himself, but still within Him. There cannot, therefore, be anyone without His Holiness, nor anyone unworthy of His perfect Love."
T-14.IV.4:5-9

Dear one, read #4. "What Is Sin?"

Lesson 251

I am in need of nothing but the truth

1. I need nothing but the truth
2. The truth satisfies all my needs
3. The truth ends all my cravings
4. The truth fulfills all my hopes
5. The truth is where I am at peace
6. Thank you, my dear Father, for your truth that sets me free

---

"Blessed are you who are willing to ask the truth of God without fear, for only thus can you learn that His answer is the release from fear."
T-11.VIII.7:7

Lesson 252

The Son of God is my Identity

1. "My Self is holy beyond all the thoughts of holiness of which I now conceive."

2. My Self is shimmering in perfect purity

3. My Self is limitless love

4. The strength of my Self comes from the Love of God Himself

5. My Self dwells with God and lives within me

6. My Self is miraculous beyond anything I can imagine

7. My Self is my truth

"Yet if truth is indivisible, your evaluation of yourself must be God's. You did not establish your value and it needs no defense. Nothing can attack it nor prevail over it. It does not vary. It merely *is*."
T-9.VIII.11:1-5

Lesson 253

My Self is ruler of the universe

1. What happens to me is by my desire
2. I rule my destiny
3. I create my world
4. I accept this and know I can always choose again
5. My Self and Your Will are one

"Unless the universe were joined in you it would be apart from God, and to be without Him *is* to be without meaning."
T-15.XI.6:6

Lesson 254

Let every voice but God's be still in me

1. I will not let ego thoughts direct my words

2. I will not let ego thoughts direct my actions

3. I see egoic thoughts as passing clouds and let them drift away

4. In silence I watch them pass

5. What is left is the Voice of God

"Clarity undoes confusion by definition, and to look upon darkness through light must dispel it."
T-11.V.2:9

Lesson 255

This day I choose to spend in perfect peace

1. I choose to be in peace today

2. Peace is God's Will for me

3. My peace is witness to my faith in God's truth

4. My peace is my gift to all my brothers

5. My peace is my gift to myself

"It is still up to you to choose to join with truth or with illusion. But remember that to choose one is to let the other go."
T-17.III.9:1-2

Lesson 256

God is the only goal I have today

1. Joining with God is the only goal I have today
2. I join with Him through forgiveness
3. I joyfully release any thoughts of sin either in myself of any of my brothers
4. Our innocence is the gift You gave us
5. My awakening is believing that this is so

"You can know God because it is His Will to be known."
T-11.VII.4:8

Lesson 257

Let me remember what my purpose is

1. My purpose is to offer God's peace to all His Sons
2. I do this through forgiveness
3. I have no will but God's
4. God is my only goal
5. Love is the gift He gives me to share
6. I am God's ambassador to the world

"Only a little wall of dust still stands between you and your brother. Blow on it lightly and with happy laughter, and it will fall away. And walk into the garden love has prepared for both of you."
T-18.VIII.13:6-8

Lesson 258

Let me remember that my goal is God

1. My goal is God

2. I willingly train my mind to overlook all little senseless goals my ego self has made

3. I gratefully replace these goals with listening to the Voice for God

4. It is here I find His Love

5. It is here I find my true Self

6. It is here I am at peace

"A Voice will answer every question you ask, and a vision will correct the perception of everything you see. For what you have made invisible is the only truth and what you have not heard is the only Answer. God would reunite you with yourself, and did not abandon you in your distress."
T.12.VIII.4:3-5

Lesson 259

Let me remember that there is no sin

1. There is no sin
2. I let go of all guilt
3. I let go of all judgments of myself and others
4. I am safe
5. We are one in God's holy Love
6. I am God's holy, sinless Son

"Your creation by God is the only Foundation that cannot be shaken, because the light is in it. Your starting point is truth, and you must return to your Beginning. Much has been seen since then, but nothing has really happened. Your Self is still in peace, even though your mind is in conflict."
T-3.VII.5:5-8

Lesson 260

Let me remember God created me

1. God created me

2. I have not left my Source

3. I am God's Son

4. This is my true Identity

5. I am sinless

6. I am holy

7. All my brothers are as myself

"God created His Sons by extending His Thought, and retaining the extensions of His Thought in His Mind. All His Thoughts are thus perfectly united within themselves and with each other."
T-6.II.8:1-2

Dear one, read #5: "What Is the Body?"

Lesson 261

God is my refuge and security

1. In God is my refuge

2. In God is my strength

3. In God is my Identity

4. In God is my peace

5. I am the holy Self that You created as your Son

6. Thank you, dear God, for keeping my holy Self eternally safe from all the idols I created

---

"The question is not how you respond to the ego, but what you believe you are. Belief is an ego function, and as long as your origin is open to belief you are regarding it from an ego viewpoint. When teaching is no longer necessary you will merely know God."
T-4.II.4:7-9

Lesson 262

Let me perceive no differences today

1. There is only one Son

2. This is all I wish to see

3. He is not a stranger to me or his Father

4. We are one in You, our Source

5. We are eternally united in Your Love

6. We are eternally the holy Son of God

"I give You thanks for what my brothers are. And as each one elects to join with me, the song of thanks from earth to Heaven grows from tiny scattered threads of melody to one inclusive chorus from a world redeemed from hell, and giving thanks to You."
T-31.VIII.11:4-5

Lesson 263

My holy vision sees all things as pure

1. The Mind of God created all that is

2. All is His Spirit

3. All is His Love

4. All is blessed with purity and joy by Him

5. With love and gratitude to my dear Father, I look on all that is

---

"To lift the veil that seems so dark and heavy, it is only needful to value truth beyond all fantasy and to be entirely unwilling to settle for illusion in place of truth."
T-16.IV.10:4

Lesson 264

I am surrounded by the Love of God

1. God's Love surrounds me

2. God's Love is in everything I touch, hear and see

3. God's Love keeps me safe

4. There is nothing that does not share God's Love

5. There is nothing that does not share God's Holiness

6. In this knowing is my safety

7. In this knowing is my peace

"Could any part of God be without His Love and could any part of His Love be contained? God is your heritage, because His one gift is Himself."
T-11.I.7:1-2

Lesson 265

Creations gentleness is all I see

1. I no longer misunderstand the world

2. I know that all fear has been in my mind

3. Today I see the world in gentleness

4. Today I see the world in its innocence

5. The light of Heaven is shining on the world

6. I am one with God

"For what is Heaven but union, direct and perfect, and without the veil of fear upon it? Here are we one looking with perfect gentleness upon each other and on ourselves."
T-20.III.10:3-4

Lesson 266

My holy Self abides in you, God's Son

1. All my brothers are my saviors

2. All of them bring Your holy voice to me

3. All of them come from the one holy Source

4. All of them were created in Love's image

5. In all of them is Your holy Name

6. We are one

"The whole reality of your relationship with Him lies in our relationship to one another. The holy instant shines alike on all relationships, for in it they *are* one. For here is only healing, already complete and perfect. For here is God, and where He is only the perfect and complete can be."
T-17.IV.16:7-10

Lesson 267

My heart is beating in the peace of God

1. I am surrounded by God's Love

2. I am surrounded by God's peace

3. Filled with God's Love and peace, I know
   my only purpose is forgiveness

4. I am God's messenger

5. His Love is my strength

6. His voice directs me

7. In Him is my home

"In the temple, Holiness waits quietly for the return of them that love it. The Presence knows they will return to purity and to grace. The graciousness of God will take them gently in, and cover all their sense of pain and loss with the immortal assurance of their Father's Love."
T-14.IX.4:1-3

Lesson 268

Let all things be exactly as they are

1. Today, I see no evil

2. Today, I hear no evil

3. Today, I speak no evil

4. Today, I seek only God's reality

5. In God's reality, I am safe

6. In God's reality, my true Self lives

"The real world is the state of mind in which the only purpose of the world is seen to be forgiveness."
T-30.V.1:1

Lesson 269

My sight goes forth to look upon Christ's face

1. I look beyond my mistakes

2. I look away from all false perceptions

3. I see my true Self

4. I see the face of the holy Son of God in everyone

5. I see my own Identity

"For you will believe in what you manifest, and as you look out so will you see in. Two ways of looking at the world are in your mind, and your perception will reflect the guidance you have chosen." T-12.VII.5:5-6

Lesson 270

I will not use the body's eyes today

1. Dear God, thank you for the gift of holy Vision

2. With this holy vision, I see a forgiven world

3. With this holy vision, I see a gracious world

4. With this holy vision, I see all your Sons

5. With this holy vision, I send blessings of peace to all the world

6. All is one in You

"If you perceive truly you are cancelling out misperceptions in yourself and in others simultaneously. Because you see them as they are, you offer them your acceptance of their truth so they can accept it for themselves. This is the healing that the miracle induces."
T-1.II.6:5-7

Dear one, read #6: "What Is the Christ?"

Lesson 271

Christ's is the vision I will use today

1. I choose what I see, hear, and am witness to

2. Today I choose to witness God's Truth in everyone I see

3. Today I look with the eyes of my true Self

4. I see the oneness of all creation

5. Thank you, dear God, for all your gifts

"Thoughts begin in the mind of the thinker, from which they reach outward. This is as true of God's Thinking as it is of yours."
T-6.II.9:1-2

Lesson 272

How can illusions satisfy God's Son?

1. Today I set all my illusions aside

2. Today I choose only the truth of who I am

3. I choose heaven

4. I choose love

5. I am your innocent, holy child

6. Thank you for showing me Your Truth and Love

"If you would be a happy learner, you must give everything you have learned to the Holy Spirit, to be unlearned for you. And then begin to learn the joyous lessons that come quickly on the firm foundation that truth is true."
T-14.II.6:1-2

Lesson 273

The stillness of the peace of God is mine

1. Dear God, Your peace is mine

2. I choose to be in Your peace today

3. I choose to dismiss any perception of disturbance

4. I see all disturbance as the opportunity to choose peace

5. In love and gratitude I share Your peace with the world

"Each of us is the light of the world, and by joining our minds in this light we proclaim the Kingdom of God together and as one."
T-6.II.13:5

Lesson 274

Today belongs to love. Let me not fear

1. Today I see only God's Truth
2. Today I hear only God's voice
3. Today I see the innocence in all my holy brother's
4. Today I create only in love
5. I am blessed as I bless

"He loves you, wholly without illusion, as you must love. For love is wholly without illusion, and therefore wholly without fear."
T-16.IV.11:8-9

Lesson 275

God's healing Voice protects all things today

1. Let me hear only God's Voice

2. In His Voice will I hear, learn and understand

3. This is where I find my healing

4. This is where I release my fear

5. In His Voice lies my peace

6. In His Voice lies the peace of the world

"You taught yourself the most unnatural habit of not communicating with your Creator. Yet you remain in close communication with Him, and with everything that is within Him, as it is within yourself. Unlearn isolation through His loving guidance, and learn of all the happy communication that you have thrown away but could not lose."
T-14.III.18:1-3

Lesson 276

The Word of God is given me to speak

1. God created me as His Son

2. I am pure

3. I am holy

4. I was created in love and in love do I create

5. This is my true Self

6. Within this Self I am sent to bless all You send to me

"In the real world there is no sickness, for there is no separation and no division. Only loving thoughts are recognized, and because no one is without your help, the Help of God goes with you everywhere. As you become willing to accept this Help by asking for It, you will give It because you want It. Nothing will be beyond your healing power, because nothing will be denied your simple request."
T-11.VIII.10:1-4

Lesson 277

Let me not bind your Son with laws I made

1. I will not condemn God's Son
2. I will not bind him with physical laws
3. He is as God created Him
4. He is made in God's image
5. I will see only the truth of him
6. I will see that he and I are one in God's loving Mind

"Temptation has one lesson it would teach, in all its forms, wherever it occurs. It would persuade the holy Son of God he is a body, born in what must die, unable to escape its frailty, and bound by what it orders him to feel. It sets the limits on what he can do; its power is the only strength he has; his grasp cannot exceed its tiny reach. Would you be this, if Christ appeared to you in all His glory, asking you but this: *Choose once again if you would take your place among the saviors of the world, or would remain in hell, and hold your brothers there.* For He *has* come, and He *is* asking this."
T-31.VIII.1:1-6

Lesson 278

If I am bound, my Father is not free

1. I willingly give up the many foolish thoughts I created about myself

2. I release the fear and unhappiness these thoughts have made

3. I see only Your truth

4. I am safe in Your Love

"The state of guiltlessness is only the condition in which what is not there has been removed from the disordered mind that thought it was. This state, and only this, must you attain, with God beside you. For until you do, you will still think that you are separate from Him."
T-14.IV.2:2-4

Lesson 279

Creations freedom promises my own

1. My freedom is here
2. I release the chains that I put upon myself
3. I awaken to God's Love
4. I accept His promises
5. I place my faith in Him alone
6. I am grateful to be free

"The ego cannot oppose the laws of God any more than you can, but it can interpret them according to what it wants, just as you can. That is why the question, 'What do you want?' must be answered."
T-5.V.6:1-2

Lesson 280

What limits can I lay upon God's Son?

1. I am free as are all Your Sons

2. I am limitless as are all your Sons

3. If I limit my brother, I limit myself

4. I honor us both as Your creation in Your Love

5. By honoring Your Son, do I honor You

"Yet you cannot be safe from truth, but only in truth. Reality is the only safety. Your will is your salvation because it is the same as God's. The separation is nothing more than the belief that it is different."
T-9.I.7:6-9

Dear one, read #7: "What Is the Holy Spirit?"

Lesson 281

I can be hurt by nothing but my thoughts

1. I will not attack myself today

2. I release all thoughts of shame

3. I release all thoughts of blame

4. I release all thoughts of guilt

5. That is not my true Self

6. I am the holy Son of God

"*Do not be afraid of the ego.* It depends on your mind, and as you made it by believing in it, so you can dispel it by withdrawing belief from it."
T-7.VIII.5:1-2

Lesson 282

I will not be afraid of love today

1. I will not allow insane thoughts to rule my mind
2. I am as God created me
3. I will not fall asleep to the truth of who I am
4. I am the Love in which I was created
5. I am that I am
6. I am the holy Son of God

"You *are* the Will of God. Do not accept anything else as your will, or you are denying what you are. Deny this and you will attack, believing you have been attacked. But see the Love of God in you, and you will see it everywhere because it *is* everywhere."
T-7.VII.10:1-4

Lesson 283

My true Identity abides in You

1. My identity is not the self I made, but the Self God made
2. This Self blesses the world
3. This Self gives true forgiveness
4. This Self loves his brothers as God does
5. I am this holy Self
6. Let me not forget my true Identity

"You are at home in God, dreaming of exile but perfectly capable of awakening to reality. Is it your decision to do so?"
T-10.I.2:1-2

Lesson 284

I can elect to change all thoughts that hurt

1. I cause my own suffering by allowing thoughts that hurt
2. I am able to choose my thoughts
3. I choose to think with the Source of Love that created me
4. I am love
5. I am joy
6. I am that I AM
7. With these thoughts do I heal the wounds of suffering

"Therefore, the first step in the undoing is to recognize that you actively decided wrongly, but can as actively decide otherwise. Be very firm with yourself in this, and keep yourself fully aware that the undoing process, which does not come from you, is nevertheless within you because God placed it there. Your part is merely to return your thinking to the point at which the error was made, and give it over to the Atonement in peace."
T-5.VII.6:3-5

Lesson 285

My holiness shines bright and clear today

1. I wake with joy
2. I expect the happy things of God to come to me
3. I invite happiness and joy
4. I accept them as I accept my holiness
5. I am as God created me
6. I am grateful for God's truth of what I am

"Love waits on welcome, not on time, and the real world is but your welcome of what always was. Therefore, the call of joy is in it, and your glad response is your awakening to what you have not lost."
T-13.VII.9:7-8

Lesson 286

The hush of Heaven holds my heart today

1. I trust in God
2. I trust that all is as it should be
3. I trust that every conflict is resolved
4. I release my meaningless need to control
5. I am at peace
6. I am in God's Love

"Your creation by God is the only Foundation that cannot be shaken, because the light is in it. Your starting point is truth, and you must return to your Beginning."
T-3.VII.5:5-6

Lesson 287

You are my goal, my Father, only You

1. I have no desire but to be one with God

2. You are my joy and happiness

3. In you does my peace abide

4. In you does my Self abide

5. I am as You created me

6. I am that I Am

"Nothing can prevail against a Son of God who commends his spirit into the Hands of his Father. By doing this the mind awakens from its sleep and remembers its Creator. All sense of separation disappears."
T-3.II.5:1-3

Lesson 288

Let me forget my Brother's past today

1. My past is forgiven

2. My brother's past is forgiven

3. We are the holy Son of God

4. We are one

5. We are equal

6. We are innocent

"But remember the first principle in this course; there is no order of difficulty in miracles. In reality you are perfectly unaffected by all expressions of lack of love. These can be from yourself and others, from yourself to others, or from others to you. Peace is an attribute *in* you. You cannot find it outside."
T-2.I.5:5-9

Lesson 289

The past is over. It can touch me not

1. I am released from my illusions of the past
2. I release all my brothers who I have imprisoned in my mind
3. We are free
4. We are innocent
5. We now live continuously in the peace and
    joy of God's holy present moment

"Let us join together in a holy instant, here in this place where
the purpose, given in a holy instant, has led you. And let us join
in faith that He Who brought us here together will offer you
the innocence you need, and that you will accept it for my love
and His."
T.19.IV.D.9:6-7

Lesson 290

My present happiness is all I see

1. In the present, I am with God

2. In God's presence is my happiness

3. In God's presence is my joy

4. In God's presence is my peace

5. In God's presence is all that I am

"The truth about you is so lofty that nothing unworthy of God is worthy of you. Choose, then, what you want in these terms, and accept nothing that you would not offer to God as wholly fitting for Him."
T-9.VII.8:4-5

Dear one, read #8: "What Is the Real World?"

Lesson 291

This is a day of stillness and peace

1. Today, I see through the eyes of the divine, one Self
2. Through the eyes of the divine Self, I see
   all things forgiven and at peace
3. I hold this vision for myself and for the world
4. In the stillness of the divine Self, my holiness blesses the world
5. In gratitude and humility, I am one with
   the Source of all creation

"Healing is release from the fear of waking and the substitution of the decision to wake. The decision to wake is the reflection of the will to love, since all healing involves replacing fear with love."
T-8.IX.5:1-2

Lesson 292

A happy outcome to all things is sure

1. There are no exceptions in what God promises

2. Joy is the guaranteed final outcome for everything

3. I release to him my small, willful thoughts
   of anger, sadness, guilt and fear

4. I accept His Will of joy and peace

5. I accept that only His Will is real

6. I thank you, dear God, that this is so

"Vision is the means by which the Holy Spirit translates your nightmares into happy dreams; your wild hallucinations that show you all the fearful outcomes of imagined sin into the calm and reassuring sights with which He would replace them. These gentle sights and sounds are looked on happily, and heard with joy. They are His substitutes for all the terrifying sights and screaming sounds the ego's purpose brought to your horrified awareness." T-20.VIII.1:4-6

Lesson 293

All fear is past and only love is here

1. All my fear is past and gone

2. Only love remains

3. Only love is eternal

4. Today I see the world with eyes of love

5. Today I see the world forgiven and holy

6. Thank You, God, for the eyes of love

"The Christ in you is very still. He looks on what He loves, and knows it as Himself. And thus does He rejoice at what He sees, because He knows that it is one with Him and with His Father."
T-24.V.1:1-3

Lesson 294

My body is a wholly neutral thing

1. I am a Son of God

2. I am eternal

3. My body is not my identity

4. My body is a neutral vehicle for my true
   Self to reside in while needed

5. When my function here is complete, I will step out of it

6. I will return to my Creator, my Source, my home

"You want communion, not the feast of fear. You want salvation, not the pain of guilt. And you want your Father, not a little mound of clay to be your home."
T-19.IV.B.4:6-8

Lesson 295

The Holy Spirit looks through me today

1. The Awakened One asks to show me
   the world through Its eyes

2. With this holy vision, I am able to see beyond
   the fearful world man has made

3. With this holy vision, I see only with love

4. With this holy vision, I am able to bless the world

5. With this holy vision is the world redeemed

"Let the Christ in you interpret for you, and do not try to limit
what you see by narrow little beliefs that are unworthy of
God's Son."
T-ll.VI.3:9

Lesson 296

The Holy Spirit speaks through me today

1. I teach today what I would learn

2. My learning goal is not conflicted

3. I listen for what the Holy Spirit would have me say and to whom

4. The Holy Spirit makes it easy for me to bless the world with Its healing words

5. The Holy Spirit shows me the path to God

"Your witnessing demonstrates your belief, and thus strengthens it. Those who witness for me are expressing, through their miracles, that they have abandoned the belief in deprivation in favor of the abundance they have learned belongs to them."
T-1.IV.4:7-8

Lesson 297

Forgiveness is the only gift I give

1. Forgiveness is the only gift I give

2. Forgiveness is the only gift I want

3. Everything I give, I give myself

4. This is salvation's simple formula

5. This is my formula for happiness and peace

6. This is the salvation of the world

"When a brother acts insanely, he is offering you an opportunity to bless him. His need is yours. You need the blessing you can offer him. There is no way for you to have it except by giving it. This is the law of God, and it has no exceptions."
T-7.VII.2:1-5

Lesson 298

I love You, Father, and I love Your Son

1. In forgiveness is the meaning of my life

2. In forgiveness is my holy sight restored

3. I willingly release all the senseless journeys, mad careers and artificial values I thought I needed to be complete

4. I am complete in loving You and all Your Sons

5. I am grateful for this truth

6. In this truth is my release

"Forgiveness removes only the untrue, lifting the shadows from the world and carrying it, safe and sure within its gentleness, to the bright world of new and clean perception. There is your purpose *now*. And it is there that peace awaits you."
T-18.IX.14:3-5

Lesson 299

Eternal holiness abides in me

1. God created me holy

2. My errors cannot dissolve my holiness

3. My illusions cannot eradicate Its eternal light

4. My holiness is guaranteed by my Creator

5. I am grateful that I am incapable of changing what God created

6. I am the holy Son of God

"Think but an instant just on this; you can behold the holiness God gave His Son. And never need you think that there is something else for you to see."
T-30.VI.9:4-6

Lesson 300

Only an instant does this world endure

1. This is my reminder to release all grievances

2. I seek only peace

3. I give only love

4. I rejoice in my true Self

5. I rejoice in knowing Your eternal Truth

6. Thank You, dear God, for my eternal holiness

"I thank You, Father, for Your perfect Son, and in his glory will I see my own."
T-30.VI.9:4-6

Dear one, read #9: "What Is the Second Coming?"

Lesson 301

And God Himself shall wipe away all tears

1. Unless I judge I cannot weep

2. Unless I judge I cannot suffer pain

3. Unless I judge I cannot feel abandoned in the world

4. I am here to bring joy, not to judge

5. I judge not and thereby release all my suffering

"Only the special could have enemies, for they are different and not the same. And difference of any kind imposes orders of reality, and a need to judge that cannot be escaped."
T-24.I.3:5-6

Lesson 302

Where darkness was I look upon the light

1. My eyes are opening at last

2. I look with my spiritual eye upon the world

3. With the eye of my higher Self, I see a world forgiven

4. With the eye of my Higher Self, I see the end of suffering

5. With the eye of my Higher Self, fear vanishes and only love remains

6. Thank you, dear Father, for the gift of holy vision

"I give you the lamp and I will go with you. You will not take this journey alone. I will lead you to your true Father, Who hath need of you, as I have. Will you not answer the call of love with joy?"
T-11.In.4:5-8

Lesson 303

The holy Christ is born in me today

1. Watch with me, angels, watch with me today

2. Let God's holy Thoughts surround me

3. Let the sounds of the world be still

4. Let me look upon all things with my spiritual eye

5. I welcome the Self you created

6. I release the self I made

7. I rest in Your holiness

"Identify with Him, and what has He that you have not? He is your eyes, your ears, your hands, your feet. How gentle are the sights He sees, the sounds He hears."
T-24.V.3:4-6

Lesson 304

Let not my world obscure the sight of Christ

1. Perception is a mirror, not a fact

2. What I look on is my state of mind reflected outward

3. I choose to look with my spiritual eye

4. I choose to forgive my brothers

5. I choose to bless the world

"You have elected to be in time rather than eternity, and therefore believe you *are* in time. Yet your election is both free and alterable. You do not belong in time. Your place is only in eternity where God Himself placed you forever."
T-5.VI.1:4-7

Lesson 305

There is a peace that Christ bestows on us

1. Father, I accept Your gift of Divine peace
2. I accept Your release from all the judgments I have put upon myself
3. I accept Your love
4. I release my guilt
5. I am saved to bless the world
6. Thank you for all you give to me

"Guilt feelings are the preservers of time. They induce fears of retaliation or abandonment, and thus ensure that the future will be like the past. This is the ego's continuity. It gives the ego a false sense of security by believing that you cannot escape from it. But you can and must."
T-5.VI.2:1-5

Lesson 306

The gift of Christ is all I seek today

1. Today I release the world I made

2. Today I release my fears

3. Today I am restored to love, to holiness, and to peace

4. Today I receive my Father's Love

5. Thank you, dear Father, for Your most precious gifts

"Let us be still an instant, and forget all things we ever learned, all thoughts we had, and every preconception that we hold of what things mean and what their purpose is. Let us remember not our own ideas of what the world is for. We do not know. Let every image held of everyone be loosened from our minds and swept away."
T-31.I.12:1-4

Lesson 307

Conflicting wishes cannot be my will

1. I am as you created me

2. May Your holy Will and my holy will be one

3. In this alignment, all my conflict is released

4. In this alignment is my peace

5. With a happy heart, I accept Your Will for me

6. Thank you, dear God, for always providing
   Your love and guidance

"Make fast your learning now, and understand you but waste time unless you go beyond what you have learned to what is yet to learn. For from this lowest point will learning lead to heights of happiness, in which you see the purpose of the lesson shining clear, and perfectly within your learning grasp."
T-31.IV.4:7-8

Lesson 308

This instant is the only time there is

1. In this instant do I find God
2. In this instant I am free
3. In this instant I am forgiven
4. In this instant I am blessed
5. In this instant I am loved
6. In this instant is Your Will revealed

"The temple you restore becomes your altar, for it was rebuilt through you."
T-14.V.10:10

Lesson 309

I will not fear to look within today

1. Within me is eternal innocence

2. Within me is the holiness of God

3. Within me is the memory of God

4. Within me is the holy altar to my Self

5. Within me is my true Identity

"You are a mirror of truth, in which God Himself shines in perfect light. To the ego's dark glass you need but say, 'I will not look there because I know these images are not true.' Then let the Holy One shine on you in peace, knowing that this and only this must be."
T-4.IV.9:1-3

Lesson 310

In fearlessness and love I spend today

1. Today I remember that God dwells within me and I am fearless

2. Today I remember that God dwells within me and I am joyous

3. Today I remember God dwells within me and I am free

4. Today I remember that God dwells within me and I am at peace

5. Thank You, dear God, for being in my heart and filling it with love

---

"The thoughts you think are in your mind, as you are in the Mind which thought of you. And so there are no separate parts in what exists within God's Mind. It is forever One, eternally united and at peace."
T-30.III.6:7-9

Dear one, read #10: "What Is the Last Judgment?"

Lesson 311

I judge all things as I would have them be

1. I lay down the heavy weight of judgment
2. I make a gift of it to God
3. I am relieved of the agony my judgments have put upon me
4. I trust that God will receive my judgments with love
5. God gives me back the gift of peace

"The Atonement is the only gift that is worthy of being offered at the altar of God, because of the value of the altar itself. It was created perfect and is entirely worthy of receiving perfection." T-2.III.5:4-5

Lesson 312

I see all things as I would have them be

1. I perceive as I have judged

2. I choose to see with the vision of my higher, holy Self

3. I choose to see through the illusions of my judgments

4. I choose to see Divine Truth

5. With this as my goal, I am set free

6. With this as my goal, the world is set free

"If you allow yourself to have in your mind only what God put there, you are acknowledging your mind as God created it. Therefore, you are accepting it as it is. Since it is whole, you are teaching peace *because* you believe in it."
T-6.5:4-6

Lesson 313

Now let a new perception come to me

1. Dear God, I ask to see with Your holy vision

2. I ask to see with love

3. I ask to see the sinlessness in all

4. I ask for true perception

5. I ask to see with the vision of my higher, holy Self

6. Thank you, dear God, for giving all that is asked

"Perhaps there is another way to look at this. What can I lose by asking?"
T-30.I.12:3-4

Lesson 314

I seek a future different from the past

1. I release the mistakes of the past
2. I choose to stay in the present
3. In this present moment is my freedom
4. In this present moment is my peace
5. I breath in the present and I breath out the past
6. I release the future to God

"Remember you made guilt, and that your plan for the escape from guilt has been to bring Atonement to it and make salvation fearful. And it is only fear that you will add if you prepare yourself for love. The preparation for the holy instant belongs to Him Who gives it. Release yourself to Him Whose function is release."
T-18.IV.6:3-5

Lesson 315

All gifts my brothers give belong to me

1. Every Son of God brings me gifts

2. In each moment there are beautiful treasures to be found

3. Words of kindness, love and gratitude that are spoken to any brother are spoken to me

4. A brother's pathway to God lights my way

5. My heart is filled with gratitude when I look on all the gifts my brother's give to me

---

"You could no more know God alone than He knows you without your brother. But together you could no more be unaware of love than love could know you not, or fail to recognize itself in you." T-18.VIII.12:4-5

Lesson 316

All gifts I give my brothers are my own

1. Every gift I give belongs to me
2. With each gift I release a past mistake
3. With each gift, God's eternal grace is give me
4. Angels watch over me and all my treasures
5. God will reveal to me the beauty of my real treasures
6. I am blessed

"The Son of God is always blessed as one. And as his gratitude goes out to you who blessed him, reason will tell you that it cannot be you stand apart from blessing. The gratitude he offers you reminds you of the thanks your Father gives you for completing Him."
T-21.VI.10:1-3

Lesson 317

I follow in the way appointed me

1. I willingly follow Your plan for me
2. I gladly go where You would have me go
3. I hear Your Voice
4. I feel Your love
5. We are one

"I am here only to be truly helpful. I am here to represent Him Who sent me. I do not have to worry about what to say or what to do, because He Who sent me will direct me. I am content to be wherever He wishes, knowing He goes there with me. I will be healed as I let Him teach me to heal."
T-2.V.18:2-6

Lesson 318

In me salvation's means and end are one

1. I am the sinless Son

2. I am the beloved Son

3. I am the holy Son

4. I am the one Son

5. I was created as the thing I seek

"All separation vanishes as holiness is shared. For holiness is power, and by sharing it, it gains in strength."
T-15.VI.3:1-2

Lesson 319

I came for the salvation of the world

1. You are the Self I sent for the salvation of the world

2. I gave you love, give it to the world

3. I gave you forgiveness, give it to the world

4. I gave you truth, give it to the world

5. I gave you peace, give it to the world

6. Rejoice in My gifts and give joy to the world

"God's plan for your salvation could not have been established without your will and your consent. It must have been accepted by the Son of God, for what God wills for him he must receive. For God wills not apart from him, nor does the Will of God wait upon time to be accomplished. Therefore, what joined the Will of God must be in you now, being eternal."
T-21.V.5:1-4

Lesson 320

My Father gives all power unto me

1. I am limitless

2. My strength is limitless

3. My peace is limitless

4. My joy is limitless

5. My love is limitless

6. All this my Father gave to me to give to the world

"Could you but realize for a single instant the power of healing that the reflection of God shining in you, can bring all the world, you could not wait to make the mirror of your mind clean to receive the image of the holiness that heals the world."
T-14.IX.7:1

Dear one, read #11: "What Is Creation?"

Lesson 321

Father, my freedom is in You alone

1. Father, Your Voice directs me to my freedom

2. You are my only Guide

3. I trust in You

4. The way to You is open and clear

5. Freedom is the choice I make today

6. Thank You for blessing me and the world with this holy gift

---

"You are not free to give up freedom, but only to deny it."
T-10.IV.5:1

Lesson 322

I can give up but what was never real

1. I willingly release all my self-made illusions
2. I willingly receive God's gifts
3. I willingly see the holy Self that was always there
4. I willingly accept God's love
5. I willingly see God's holiness

"Earth can reflect Heaven or hell; God or the ego. You need but leave the mirror clean and clear of all the images of hidden darkness you have drawn upon it. God will shine upon it of Himself. Only the clear reflection of Himself can be perceived upon it."
T-14.IX.5:4-7

Lesson 323

I gladly make the "sacrifice" of fear

1. I gladly give up all suffering
2. I gladly give up all sense of loss and sadness
3. I gladly give up all anxiety and doubt
4. I freely let God's love come into my awareness
5. I freely accept God's eternal joy

"Your 'evil' thoughts that haunt you now will seem increasingly remote and far away from you. And they go farther and farther off, because the sun in you has risen that they may be pushed away before the light. They linger for a while, a little while, in twisted forms too far away for recognition, and are gone forever. And in the sunlight you will stand in quiet, in innocence and wholly unafraid."
T-25.IV.4:4-7

Lesson 324

I merely follow, for I would not lead

1. Father, you gave me the plan for my salvation

2. You have told me what I must do

3. The path to Your love and peace is clear

4. I willingly follow the path you clearly set

5. I know that if I stray, Your loving Voice will lead me back

---

"There is a resting place so still no sound except a hymn to Heaven rises up to gladden God the Father and the Son. Where Both abide are They remembered, Both. And where They are is Heaven and is peace."
T-29.V.1:3-5

Lesson 325

All things I think I see reflect ideas

1. What I see reflects what I want

2. From what I want comes an image

3. I project the image outward

4. The world I see is what I created

5. Let me want only a forgiving, loving
   world filled with the joy of God

6. Let me reflect only that only that to my brothers

"And love would prove all suffering is but a vain imagining, a foolish wish with no effects. Your health is a result of your desire to see your brother with no blood upon his hands, nor guilt upon his heart made heavy with the proof of sin. And what you wish is given you to see."
T-27.II.7:6-8

Lesson 326

I am forever an Effect of God

1. I was created in the Mind of God

2. God is my Cause

3. I am God's Effect

4. All God's attributes abide in me

5. God has endowed me with creative power

6. With His gifts I create love, joy and peace

7. This is my purpose

"To love yourself is to heal yourself and you cannot perceive part of you as sick and achieve your goal. Brother, we heal together as we live together and love together."
T-11.VIII.11:3-4

Lesson 327

I need but call and You will answer me

1. God hears my call

2. He Himself answers me

3. I place my faith in Him

4. I trust His eternal promise

5. I judge it not

6. This is my road to salvation

7. This is my road to peace

"The Thought God holds of you is like a star, unchangeable in an eternal sky. So high in Heaven is it set that those outside of Heaven know not it is there. Yet still and white and lovely will it shine through all eternity. There was no time it was not there, no instant when its light grew dimmer or less perfect ever was." T-30.III.8:4-7

Lesson 328

I choose the second place to gain the first

1. I no longer seek to control my world

2. God's will is first, not mine

3. God's Voice is first, not mine

4. I listen, He directs

5. I am relieved from all I thought I had to do

6. I am at peace

7. Thank you, dear God, for Your divine direction

"The first rule, then, is not coercion, but a simple statement of a simple fact. You will not make decisions by yourself whatever you decide. For they are made with idols or with God. And you ask help of anti-Christ or Christ, and which you choose will join with you and tell you what to do."
T-30.I.14:6-9

Lesson 329

I have already chosen what You will

1. I am Your Will extended and extending

2. I am one with You eternally

3. I am safe

4. I am untroubled and serene

5. I am in endless joy

6. I am one with all creation

"Those who would let illusions be lifted from their minds are this world's saviors, walking the world with their Redeemer, and carrying His message of hope and freedom and release from suffering to everyone who needs a miracle to save him."
T-22.IV.6:5

Lesson 330

I will not hurt myself again today

1. Today I am willing to accept forgiveness as my only function

2. I am willing to accept God's power into my mind

3. I am willing to accept God's love

4. I am willing to release my suffering and accept God's gift of freedom and joy

5. I am willing to accept my true Self in place of all that I have made

6. I am willing to accept that I am one with God

"Who would be willing to be turned away from all the roadways of the world, unless he understood their real futility? Is it not needful that he should begin with this, to seek another way instead?"
T-31.IV.5:1-2

Dear one, read #12: "What Is the Ego?"

Lesson 331

There is no conflict, for my will is Yours

1. I am loved by God, my creator

2. I am one with Him

3. I accept that His will is the Will of Love

4. I awaken from the fearful dream I made and find Your peace

5. I am willing to forgive so that I may dwell with You

6. May Your Will and my will be one

"God but ensured that you would never lose your will when
He gave you His perfect Answer. Hear it now, that you may be
reminded of His Love and learn your will."
T-30.II.2:6-7

Lesson 332

Fear binds the world. Forgiveness sets it free

1. I willingly release all the fantasies I made about the world
2. I awaken to Truth
3. In Truth is forgiveness which I willingly receive and give
4. Here is my freedom from all the fear I made
5. With love and gratitude, I offer this freedom to the world

---

"Nothing can be caused without some form of union, be it with a dream of judgment or the Voice for God. Decisions cause results *because* they are not made in isolation. They are made by you and your adviser, for yourself and for the world as well. The day you want you offer to the world, for it will be what you have asked for, and will reinforce the rule of your adviser in the world."
T-30.I.16:4-7

Lesson 333

Forgiveness ends the dream of conflict here

1. I am willing to resolve all conflicts I have created in my mind

2. I accept conflict as mine to resolve and not something to be projected outward

3. I am willing to release my defenses of specialness and separation that keep my conflicts alive

4. I am willing to end my suffering

5. I invite forgiveness in for myself and for all my brothers

6. Through this resolve is peace brought to the world

"In honesty, is it not harder for you to say 'I love' than 'I hate'? You associate love with weakness and hatred with strength, and your own real power seems to you as your real weakness. For you could not control your joyous response to the call of love if you heard it, and the whole world you thought you made would vanish."
T-13.III.3:1-3

Lesson 334

Today I claim the gifts forgiveness gives

1. I follow Your map of forgiveness and find Your treasures

2. I find peace

3. I find love

4. I find joy

5. I find sinlessness

6. I am grateful for all Your precious gifts

"As God ascends into His rightful place and you to yours, you will experience again the meaning of relationship and know it to be true. Let us ascend in peace together to the Father, by giving Him ascendance in our minds. We will gain everything by giving Him the power and the glory, and keeping no illusions of where they are."
T-17.IV.16:1-3

Lesson 335

I choose to see my brother's sinlessness

1. Forgiveness is the choice I make
2. I choose to see with my spiritual eye
3. I choose to see my brother's sinlessness
4. I choose to see his holiness
5. In him I find my Self
6. We are one with each other and with God

"You will not see the symbol of your brother's guiltlessness shining within him while you still believe it is not there. His guiltlessness is *your* Atonement. Grant it to him, and you will see the truth of what you have acknowledged."
T-14.IV.1:3-5

Lesson 336

Forgiveness lets me know that minds are joined

1. I forgive in-order to end my false
   perceptions of separation and sin
2. I forgive in-order to uncover the altar to the truth
3. I forgive in-order to restore my mind to peace
4. I forgive that I may dwell with God
5. I forgive that I may love

"The secret of salvation is but this: that you are doing this unto yourself."
T-27.VIII.10:1

Lesson 337

My sinlessness protects me from all harm

1. My sinlessness ensures me perfect peace

2. My sinlessness ensures me eternal safety

3. My sinlessness ensures me everlasting love

4. My sinlessness ensures me complete deliverance from suffering

5. I accept my higher, holy Self

6. I am the Son my Father loves

"Yet if truth is indivisible, your evaluation of yourself must *be* God's. You did not establish your value and it needs no defense. Nothing can attack it nor prevail over it. It does not vary. It merely *is*."
T-9.VIII.11:1-5

Lesson 338

I am affected only by my thoughts

1. I choose my thoughts

2. I choose to replace thoughts of fear with thoughts of love

3. I choose to replace thoughts of judgment
   with thoughts of sinlessness

4. I choose to replace thoughts of conflict with thoughts of peace

5. I choose to replace thoughts of illusion
   with thoughts of God's Truth

6. Thank You, dear God, for allowing me to
   choose holy, healing thoughts

---

*"I am responsible for what I see. I choose the feelings I
experience, and I decide upon the goal I would achieve. And
everything that seems to happen to me I ask for, and receive as I
have asked."*
T-21.II.2:3-5

Lesson 339

I will receive whatever I request

1. I no longer choose to think pain is pleasure
2. I no longer fear joy
3. I no longer ask for what, in the end, brings me suffering
4. I choose to ask for what I really want
5. I choose to ask for God's love, God's peace, and God's joy
6. In gratitude I am open to receive God's precious gifts

"As you look in, you choose the guide for seeing. And then you look out and behold his witnesses. This is why you find what you seek. What you want in yourself you will make manifest, and you will accept it from the world because you put it there by wanting it."
T-12.VII.7:2-5

Lesson 340

I can be free of suffering today

1. Today I choose to be free of suffering

2. Today I choose to hear the Voice of forgiveness

3. Today I choose freedom

4. Today I choose joy

5. Today I am glad for my release

6. I am grateful for the holiness of today

"No one who hears His answer but will give up insanity. For His answer is the reference point beyond illusions, from which you can look back on them and see them as insane. But seek this place and you will find it, for Love is in you and will lead you there."
T-13.III.12:8-10

Dear one, read #13: "What Is a Miracle?"

Lesson 341

I can attack but my own sinlessness,
And it is only that which keeps me safe

1. I am holy

2. I am one with You

3. I am the receiver of Your deepest love

4. I am Your creation

5. I am sinless

"For in the holy instant, free of the past, you see that love is in you, and you have no need to look without and snatch love guiltily from where you thought it was."
T-15.V.9:7

Lesson 342

I let forgiveness rest upon all things,
For thus forgiveness will be given me

1. The hell I made is not real
2. I have the key that proves its unreality
3. I have the key to heaven's door
4. The key is forgiveness
5. Today I choose to open the door
6. I choose to stand in Your truth

"God knows you *now*. He remembers nothing, having always known you exactly as He knows you now. The holy instant reflects His knowing by bringing all perception out of the past, thus removing the frame of reference you have built by which to judge your brothers."
T-15.V.9:1-3

Lesson 343

I am not asked to make a sacrifice
To find the mercy and the peace of God

1. God has given me the gift of everything

2. I give to others as God has given me

3. Thus do I complete a sacred, eternal circle

4. This is my function here

5. This is my salvation

"To teach the whole Sonship without exception demonstrates that you perceive its wholeness, and have learned that it is one."
T-6.V.C.8:1

Lesson 344

Today I learn the law of love; that what I give my brother is my gift to me

1. What I give my brother is my gift to me

2. I accept that this is God's law

3. I choose to have the wealth of heaven's treasures

4. I give my brothers forgiveness

5. I give my brothers love

6. In fulfilling God's law do I grow close to Him

"Love is not an illusion. It is a fact. Where disillusionment is possible there was not love but hate. For hate *is* an illusion, and what can change was never love."
T-16.IV.4:1-4

Lesson 345

I offer only miracles today,
For I would have them be returned to me

1. I have been sent here to be God's miracle worker

2. I offer my brother's the miracle of love

3. I offer my brother's the miracle of forgiveness

4. I offer my brother's the miracle of peace

5. As I offer these gifts, they are returned to me

6. Thus is the world blessed and made holy

"The world is very tired, because it is the idea of weariness. Our task is the joyous one of waking it to the Call for God."
T-5.II.10:6-7

Lesson 346

Today the peace of God envelops me, And I forget all things except His Love

1. Today I choose to let love correct my perception of all things
2. Today I look with the spiritual eye of my higher Self
3. Today I look beyond form and time
4. With my higher Self as my guide, I breath in Your eternal love
5. Today I know Your peace

"Do you prefer that you be right or happy? Be you glad that you are told where happiness abides, and seek no longer elsewhere. You will fail. But it is given you to know the truth, and not to seek for it outside yourself."
T-29.VII.1:9-12

Lesson 347

Anger must come from judgment.
Judgment is the weapon I would use against myself,
To keep the miracle away from me.

1. My anger comes from my judgments

2. Judgment is not God's will, but my own

3. I am willing to practice non-judgment

4. When I feel a judgment arise, I stop and I
   release it to the Holy Spirit within

5. The Holy Spirit transforms my judgment to love

6. Through this practice do Your miracles come to me

"If you would remember your Father, let the Holy Spirit order your thoughts and give only the answer with which He answers you."
T-14.X.10-4

Lesson 348

I have no cause for anger or for fear,
For You surround me. And in every need
That I perceive, Your grace suffices me.

1. I willingly release my anger

2. I willingly release my fear

3. I would rather have God's peace and joy

4. I would rather share God's holiness

5. I am safe

6. I am loved always

"The Holy Spirit atones in all of us by undoing, and thus lifts the burden you have placed in your mind. By following Him you are led back to God where you belong, and how can you find the way except by taking your brother with you?"
T-5.IV.6:1-2

Lesson 349

Today I let Christ's vision look upon
All things for me and judge them not, but give
Each one a miracle of love instead

1. Today I look with my spiritual eye

2. My spiritual eye does not judge what it sees

3. My spiritual eye beholds everything with love

4. Looking with my spiritual eye, I bless the world

5. Looking with my spiritual eye, my mind is healed

6. Looking with my spiritual eye, I know I am free

"A miracle is a service. It is the maximal service you can render to another. It is a way of loving your neighbor as yourself. You recognize your own and your neighbor's worth simultaneously."
T-1.I.18:1-4

Lesson 350

Miracles mirror God's eternal Love.
To offer them is to remember Him
And through His memory to save the world

1. As I forgive, I am purified

2. As I walk and talk in memory of Him, I am purified

3. As I am purified, I am able to see my brother's purity

4. We are the holy, sinless Sons of God

5. We are held in each moment by His Love

6. With humility and with deep gratitude, I accept my purification

---

"Miracles should inspire gratitude, not awe. You should thank God for what you really are. The children of God are holy and the miracle honors their holiness, which can be hidden but never lost."
T-1.I.31:1-3

Dear one, read #14: "What Am I?"

Lesson 351

My sinless brother is my guide to peace
My sinful brother is my guide to pain
And which I choose to see I will behold

1. Every brother is God's holy Son
2. I choose to see the eternal, holy Self in all my brothers
3. I choose to see the eternal, holy Self in me
4. I am he and he is me
5. Neither of us is separate or alone
6. Together, we are one

"Yet this world is only in the mind of its maker, along with his real salvation. Do not believe it is outside of yourself, for only by recognizing where it is will you gain control over it. For you do have control over your mind, since the mind is the mechanism of decision."
T-12.III.9:8-10

Lesson 352

Judgment and love are opposites. From one Comes all the sorrows of the world. But from The other comes the peace of God Himself

1. I choose to look with the eye of forgiveness
2. I choose to see the sinless Son of God
3. I choose to see with love
4. With the memory of You and the heart of my higher Self is this done
5. I am the peace of God
6. I am the salvation of the world

"Forgiveness is your peace, for herein lies the end of separation and the dream of danger and destruction, sin and death; of madness and of murder, grief and loss. This is the 'sacrifice' salvation asks, and gladly offers peace instead of this."
T-29.VI.1:4-5

Lesson 353

My eyes, my tongue, my hands, my feet today Have but one purpose; to be given Christ To use to bless the world with miracles

1. I am joined with the I Am presence

2. My purpose is to be of service however I am led

3. I am the one the world is waiting for

4. I am the pure, sinless Self which some may call the Christ

5. I am here to bless the world with miracles

"All miracles mean life, and God is the Giver of life. His Voice will direct you very specifically. You will be told all you need to know."
T-1.I.4:1-3

Lesson 354

We stand together, Christ and I, in peace And certainty of purpose. And in Him Is His Creator, as He is in me

1. I am the holy Son of God

2. I choose to express my holy Self in all I do and say

3. I choose to remember who I truly am

4. I choose to release the self I made and be the Self You created

5. May You guide me, dear Beloved One, to always choose for peace, love and forgiveness

6. Thank You

"What seemed once to be a special problem, a mistake without a remedy, or an affliction without a cure, has been transformed into a universal blessing. Sacrifice is gone. And in its place the Love of God can be remembered, and will shine away all memory of sacrifice and loss."
T-26.II.7:5-7

Lesson 355

There is no end to all the peace and joy
And all the miracles that I will give,
When I accept God's Word. Why not today?

1. I accept God's Word

2. I am His sinless Son

3. I am eternal

4. I am Holy

5. I am one with the I Am presence

6. Love, joy and peace are mine

7. I give them to the world

"An empty space that is not seen as filled, an unused interval of time not seen as spent and fully occupied, become a silent invitation to the truth to enter, and to make itself at home. No preparation can be made that would enhance the invitation's real appeal. For what you leave as vacant God will fill, and where He is there must the truth abide."
T-27.III.4:1-3

Lesson 356

Sickness is but another name for sin
Healing is but another name for God
The miracle is thus a call to Him

1. God's promise is to me

2. I am nothing I thought I was, but everything he created

3. I am sinless and beyond suffering

4. I am the Self He created in His image

5. I call to Him and He answers me

6. I am the Son He loves so dearly

"And they will look upon the vision of the Son of God, remembering who he is they sing of. What is a miracle but this remembering? And who is there in whom this memory lies not? The light in one awakens it in all. And when you see it in your brother, you *are* remembering for everyone."
T-20.I.10:3-7

Lesson 357

Truth answers every call we make to God
Responding first with miracles, and then
Returning unto us to be itself

1. I have imprisoned myself in my mind

2. Forgiveness of my brother is the golden key

3. I forgot to see my brother's holiness

4. Therefore, I forgot to see my holiness

5. I hear Your voice instructing me: "Behold
   his sinlessness, and be you healed"

"The meaning of love is lost in any relationship that looks to weakness, and hopes to find love there. The power of love, which *is* its meaning, lies in the strength of God that hovers over it and blesses it silently by enveloping it in healing wings. Let this be, and do not try to substitute your 'miracle' for this."
T-16.I.6:1-3

Lesson 358

No call to God can be unheard nor left Unanswered. And of this I can be sure; His answer is the one I really want

1. I am always answered by God

2. All I am is created by Him

3. All I have is exactly in the form chosen for me

4. I cannot judge, as I cannot see in all directions of time and space

5. I am still and know His Love for me

6. I am still and know my Self

"A sense of separation from God is the only lack you really need correct."
T.1.VI.2:1

Lesson 359

God's answer is some form of peace. All pain Is healed; all misery replaced with joy. All prison doors are opened. And all sin Is understood as merely a mistake.

1. I willingly accept that I have misunderstood all things

2. I willingly accept my sinlessness

3. I willingly see that my mistakes have no eternal effect on my sinlessness

4. This understanding extends to all God's Sons

5. With this acceptance do I forgive myself and all my brothers

6. With this understanding am I at peace

"*You* know what your Creator wills is possible, but what you made believes it is not so. Now must you choose between yourself and an illusion of yourself. Not both, but one. There is no point in trying to avoid this one decision. It must be made. Faith and belief can fall to either side, but reason tells you misery lies only on one side and joy upon the other."
T-22.II.6:5-10

Lesson 360

Peace be to me, the holy Son of God.
Peace be to my brother, who is one with me.
Let all the world be blessed with peace through us.

1. I am Your Son as You created me
2. I am holy
3. I am sinless
4. I am one with all my brothers in Your eternal peace
5. I am grateful to know Your Truth
6. With humbleness and deep love do I accept Your Love

"Without you there would be a lack in God, a Heaven incomplete, a Son without a Father. There could be no universe and no reality. For what God wills is whole, and part of Him because His Will is One."
T-24.VI.2:1-3

Lessons 361-365

This holy instant would I give to You.
Be You in charge. For I would follow You,
Certain that Your direction gives me peace.

1. Love surrounds me

2. God's angels surround me

3. I am never alone

4. I am never without guidance

5. I ask and it is given

6. I matter to Him and to the world

7. In deep gratitude do I complete this lesson

8. Thank You, dear God, Master Jesus, the Divine Spirit within, and all my holy teachers on earth and beyond

9. I am blessed

"How can you who are so holy suffer? All your past except its beauty is gone, and nothing is left but a blessing. I have saved all your kindnesses and every loving thought you ever had. I have purified them of the errors that hid their light, and kept them for you in their perfect radiance. They are beyond destruction and beyond guilt. They came from the Holy Spirit within you, and we know what God creates is eternal. You can indeed depart in peace because I have loved you as I loved myself. You go with my blessing and for my blessing. Hold it and share it, that it may always be ours. I place the peace of God in your heart and in your hands, to hold and share. The heart is pure to hold it, and the hands are strong to give it. We cannot lose. My judgment is as strong as the wisdom of God, in Whose Heart and Hands we have our being. His quiet children are His blessed Sons. The Thoughts of God are with you."

T-5.IV.8:1-14

Acknowledgements

What a challenge it is to sit down and write about all the people that deserve acknowledgement. In order to do that I would, of necessity, have to go back to childhood; to the people who shaped my life and, for whatever the reason, drove me to study spirituality. They created the drive and the thirst, while many teachers along the way pointed me to where I am now in my spiritual journey. Therefore, I will direct my acknowledgements to those who I feel have been more directly involved in my creating this book.

With deep appreciation…

To my dear friend, Evonne Weinhaus, a fellow author, who understands the challenges, blocks, and frustrations of writing. As I wrote this book, Evonne was always there to listen, encourage, and gently critique. Her continuous willingness to lend support and guidance was invaluable in motivating me on to the completion of this work.

To Ruth Hanna, a gentle, loving soul, who introduced me to the *Course* and lived her life to be an example of its teachings. I do not think I would have gone so deeply into the *Course* if it had not been for the loving guidance of Ruth.

To all the wonderful *Course* teachers who have generously shared their love and understanding of the *Course* freely with us as well as the many, many students that I have had the honor to study with. And, to my dear students as well; you always make me dig deeper into the material and myself. Some of all of you are in this book.

To my dear friend and teacher Michael Shapiro who I had the privilege to study mystical Judaism with for many years. Although the language was different, Michael taught me the essence of the *Course* teachings.

To my dear husband, Bob Siegel who is not a *Course* student, but has always been supportive of my studies and, on those days when I was stuck or wondering if I should even be writing this book, Bob would listen and encourage me to move on. As I started typing up the work and formatting it, etc., Bob was always there to help me on the technical end, which was much appreciated as my computer skills, especially when I started out, were, shall we say, rather lacking.

Of course, one could not write anything about *A Course in Miracles* without a deep thank you to Helen Schucman and William Thetford, the scribes of the *Course*. Little did you know when you started your work together what it would come to mean to millions of us all over the world. May your memory be as blessed as you have blessed us.

And finally, to my mother Annette Theresa Goodman, who searched and searched for a spiritual meaning to her life, but could not find it. Perhaps she was the motivation, albeit subconsciously, for me to continue the search. Unfortunately, The *Course* came after her short time in this world. I know she would have loved it.

Love and Blessings to you all.

Barbara Goodman Siegel

Barbara Goodman Siegel, O.M.C., is an ordained ministerial counselor, nationally published author and teacher. Prior to becoming a ministerial counselor, Barbara was a career consultant and author. Her book, *The 5 Secrets to Finding a Job* (Impact Publications, 1994) was based on her experience as a career consultant. Barbara is proud to say that her book was used in the first federally funded virtual program that reached high school and college students as well as prison inmates ready to go back into the job market. Barbara was a sought-after speaker on the art of finding a job and appeared on national media from New York to Los Angeles. She also wrote career search articles for the St. Louis Post Dispatch.

Soon after Barbara's book was published, she was introduced by a friend to *A Course in Miracles*. That, she says, was a life changing experience and she became a dedicated student. A year later, she had a unique opportunity to study Jewish mysticism with a well renowned teacher. Even though the language used in these two teachings was different, Barbara saw that both were reflecting the same truths.

After several years of studying the *Course* and Jewish mysticism, Barbara felt a strong pull to redirect her own career into spiritual counseling, teaching, and writing. She became an ordained ministerial counselor through Pathways of Light, a non-denominational spiritual college with teachings based on ACIM. Barbara was ordained in 2010 and since then she has been able to fulfil her desire to teach, write for spiritual publications, and provide non-denominational spiritual counseling.

Barbara lives in St. Louis, MO with her husband Bob and their rescue cat, Mitzy. She continues to be a devoted student of the *Course*. She engages in many in-person and on-line teachings and retreats related to the *Course* (as well as other spiritual material), and enjoys long walks where she can commune with all of God's wonderful creation.

You can reach Barbara at:
Barbara@BarbaraGoodmanSiegel.com